Fierce

CONQUERING THE BATTLEGROUND
BETWEEN WHO YOU ARE AND
WHO YOU'RE DESTINED TO BE

KATLYN A. DAVIS

Design by Vanessa Mendozzi

ISBN Ebook: 978-1-7366731-1-9
ISBN Paperback: 978-1-7366731-2-6
ISBN Hardback: 978-1-7366731-0-2

Contents

PART I: Self-Awareness

PART II: Growth

PART III: Intentionality

PART IV: Confidence

FORWARD

When someone says, "I am writing a book," most of us smile and nod with politeness, and we may even ask what it is about. Rarely do we expect the person to complete the book. It is extremely difficult to put an entire series of thoughts about a specific topic together in a cogent manner that might offer some illumination to others. I have started many books but have only published a few. It is no small task. The fact that Katlyn Davis not only wrote a book but wrote one so comprehensive and thoughtful is nothing short of inspiring.

My name is J. Wesley Mullins, but you can call me Wes. I am the author of *Unabashedly Resolute: The Chasm*. It is a primer for Christian Apologetics and Critical Thinking. I also published a book of poetry, *Seasons of Melancholy,* a vulnerable portrait of masculinity. My educational credentials began at the University of South Carolina with a B.A. in English Literature in 2009. I hold two certifications in Christian Apologetics: one from Biola University (2014), and one from The OCCA (The Oxford Centre of Christian Apologetics — 2018). I also hold a Certification of Theological Studies from the University of Oxford (2018) and was a member of the C.S. Lewis Society of Oxford (2018).

All of this and yet the greatest education I have received has been self-education from the works of Lewis, Frankl, Peterson, Solzhenitsyn, Ten Boom, Doyle, etc., and from everyday life. Life is a fantastic teacher if you take time to pay attention. My professional life includes an international photography business for twelve years with my wife. I was a corporate trainer for a national healthcare conglomerate for nearly five years, and recently, I founded Unabashedly Resolute Institute (an educational institution that promotes critical thinking in all areas of life). Personally, I have survived cancer, bullying, self-sabotage, two bad car accidents, the death of my father, and bad philosophy/theology… in no particular order of hierarchy. My wife and I have been married for seventeen years, which I think actually affords me great wisdom in the study of myself. I have found being married is living in a state of perpetual vulnerability; there is nowhere to hide. Being a father of precocious and brilliant twins keeps me humble and honest, wherein I have to continually push myself to be better and better informed. It is a privilege to pass down to them the greatest piece of advice I was ever given by my father, "Don't believe people because they say it's true. Study for yourself, try to prove them wrong, try to prove yourself wrong. If you can't... then you might be right." These are truly words to live by and words my good friend Katlyn lives by as proof of this book.

I met Katlyn at an organization called CSF (Christian Student Fellowship) at the University of Kentucky after a lecture I gave on Christian Apologetics. I happened to have a copy of my book on hand, and it found its way into her hands. I saw her a few times after, and she would always mention the book and how it helped her. As an author, there is no reward greater than to have your readers' thanks and gratitude for putting something into writing that helped them.

It was a few years later when I was beginning a literary group called Verum Fabula Fellowship (VFF), that she actually became a part of my life. It is where she became family. I had sent her an invitation to VFF on a whim. Knowing she had liked my book, I thought maybe she would like more of the same. She told me later that it was not the attraction of apologetics or literature that enticed her; rather, it was my last line of the email, "Bring your personal heresies and vices." I always include some sort of line like that. It's to let people know that you are welcome to come and wrestle out life. It is a place for questions – to learn to ask better questions. We do not have all the answers yet; we do not yet "have faces" and are "man-shaped stain" still living in the shadowlands; the land of answers is yet to come. She was hungry for what we offered – an honest place without religious and social taboos. We all have a lot to learn from each other, and it would be utter stupidity and hubris to think otherwise.

Her contribution to VFF and our weekly meetings was felt instantly; she was not shy about making her opinions known. She courageously engaged in vigorous debate, not because she was argumentative, but rather because she was desperate (as she points out in her book). She was lost, suffering, and in pain. And the only way forward was to wrestle the truth out of her questions. Success would require a Jacob experience – to become Israel.

The Katlyn I know today is not the Katlyn I met in 2019. She found salve for those wounds in the words of C.S. Lewis, Tolkien, and others. From the moment we met, I have never worried about her or the trajectory of her life. It was clear she is not afraid of a fight, especially if the fight is internal. To battle the "Watchful Dragons" of her mind, to quell the chaos of erratic and neurotic thoughts and emerge a true Dragon Tamer, Katlyn is the exact type of person we both wanted and needed in VFF.

It will come of no surprise once you read the book that Katlyn is not regurgitating or parroting psychobabble or pseudo-intellectual arguments she gleaned from a Ted Talk or social media bingeing. She has done her homework. There are references and well-reasoned conclusions from high-level academic works to popular authors as well as theological, historical, political, and literary references. The research is vast and well-rounded. What she is offering is a process in the form of a personal thesis. It is a refining process that she endured and emerged from the other side resolute. Some self-help gurus offer mantras, incorporated information, and commercialized propaganda. Katlyn does not. She has ripped open her heart and dumped it onto the pages, and then used the tools of reason and imagination to paint a portrait worth your time to contemplate. She unabashedly tells you who she is, what her situation was, and what she did to repair her mind and environment. The vulnerability in this book is indicative of earned wisdom, not encouraging rhetoric. Most people will not understand what it is to do the hard work of ripping apart your worldview, rebuilding it, and then being able to articulate how you did it. It takes a level of intentionality and self-awareness that is rare. Just the amount of reading and thinking required to write this book is impressive for anyone, let alone someone as young as Katlyn. The concepts she tackles with personal stories and accessible syntax proves that she has been actively imbibing information, distilling it down, and then repeating the process again and again. One does not get to the level of ease of expression Katlyn offers without constant proximity and mastery of the content.

It was an honor to get to read this book prior to release and be able to write this forward. The fact that she trusts me with her dream, her book, her idea, is a genuine mark of friendship.

I can't recommend this book enough. It's real, raw, and authentic; you cannot ask any more of a book or an author. Her calm tone and encouraging voice, even when she is being tough, keeps the reader engaged and hanging on to what is coming next. It was a joy to read from beginning to end.

Having said all that, is everything in the following pages *the* Truth? Will it answer all your questions and wipe away all your anxiety? Or do I even agree with her on everything in this book? No. There is no such book; it does not exist. This book is not meant to give you the answers. It is to help you wrestle out better questions so you can get your life together. So you can aim more precisely at your target. It is a call to action, to a responsibility that will breed success. She is offering a long, hard stare at yourself through the struggles of her own life. Take from it what helps you, leave the rest. She is giving this to you as a true meaning of an author, "Here is what I have gone through, here is what I did to overcome, maybe this will help you do the same."

So open your mind, open your heart, and see what can be learned from this courageous DOER of a woman.

J. Wesley Mullins

Author of *Unabashedly Resolute: The Chasm*

Founder of Verum Fabula Fellowship & Unabashedly Resolute Institute

PREFACE

This book might be for you, but it may not be.

This book might be like any other self-help book you've read, or it may change your life with its gold nuggets scattered throughout that are intended to make you question your current habits, lifestyle choices, the way you process information, and what makes you, you.

This book might be too personal for you, or maybe not personal enough.

I can only assure you that rawness, transparency, passion, and pure love were poured into the creation of this book. It was written in moments of grief like no other, joy unfathomable, and every emotion in between. It was written on the beach, in the mountains, near a rainforest, and by the desert. It was written in foreign lands, where I call home, and the clouds in between. It was given up on and courageously begun again.

I can only hope that you take it for what it is—a journey of self-awareness, growth, intentionality, and confidence. Each one relying on the prior to continue the cycle onward.

To everyone who has been a part of my life—whether for only a moment, months, or years—you are part of what has made me the person I am today. Without your influence and impact, this book wouldn't be what it is.

Thank you to those who have loved me, challenged me, left me, and found me. All of you will forever be a part of my story.

But a special thank you to those who have stayed or have just decided to come along for the ride.

This is just the beginning.

INTRODUCTION

Hey, I'm Katlyn!
I'm too young, too inexperienced, too a lot of things to be writing this book. But here I am, writing this book. I'm tired of seeing people who use "I'm too _____" as their excuse for not chasing their dreams and accomplishing the impossible. I'm also tired of seeing people cling to fear, refuse to evolve into the people they were created to be, and fall short of reaching their potential.

Based on the introspection I have done, wisdom from life experience, and having mentors and community that challenge me day in and day out, I have come up with four pillars that I believe are the keys to transforming you from the person you are to the person you were destined to be.

Self-Awareness
Growth
Intentionality
Confidence

Each of these pillars isolated is not enough. It takes all four to reap the reward of true inward transformation.

Why should you trust me to guide you down the path towards transformation? That's what I would be asking if I were you, and I have a few reasons.

I am a first-generation college student who grew up in one of the poorest towns in eastern Tennessee. Statistically speaking, I wasn't supposed to go very far (metaphorically and physically). Where I come from, you stay where you were raised. I graduated high school and decided to move to Kentucky to pursue a degree that I thought was way above my level of intelligence. I finished school with a 3.7 GPA and landed my dream first job at the headquarters of a Fortune 1000 company you may have heard of called Valvoline. I never flew on my first plane until I was almost twenty years old, and now at twenty-three I have traveled to fifteen countries. I am twenty-three years old (twenty-four when this book is published) and am writing my first novel all while working a full-time job, going back to graduate school, and taking care of an extra-large Newfoundland puppy named Roman Beau. You could say I'm really good at beating the odds and daring to do the unlikely and maybe even the impossible.

I've learned that my fear of failure is great, but my fear of not trying is even greater. I knew as a little girl I was destined for something special. I loved my tiny town but knew there was more out there if I could ever just find it. I had an aching inside of me telling me that there were many people, places, passions, and dreams I would soon love if only I could get out and find them—so I did.

I've done a lot in my twenty-three years of life. I hope some of my adventurous travel stories, college stories, relationship stories, and typical Katlyn crazy stories can at least give you something to look forward to with every turned page.

And I can promise you two things:

- There is more life out there to be lived for you—and to be lived *well.*
- There's a battleground standing between who you are and who you're destined to be—don't quit fighting just yet.

Love always,

Katlyn

PART I

Self-Awareness

SOMETIMES IN LIFE, OUR GAZE IS SO FOCUSED ON OUR DREAMS THAT ALONG THE WAY, WE LOSE SIGHT OF THE MAN OR WOMAN WHO DECIDED TO BEGIN THE JOURNEY OF THE DREAM IN THE FIRST PLACE.

WHO AM I?

When I decided I wanted to write this book, it wasn't because I had all of the chapters planned or that I was inspired beyond belief. When I decided to write this book, I was going through one of the lowest points of my life. I had never felt so misguided, broken, confused, and unsure of what the future held. Everything I thought was true turned out to be only a figment of my imagination. My plans for the future were ripped out from under me, and I was left with nothing but doubt, fear, and disappointment.

It's imperative to have goals and plans, but there isn't a worse feeling than when the dreams you have intentionally invested so much in crumble right in front of your eyes and, even worse, without any rhyme or reason. When we go through adversity, we begin to question everything. Our doubts begin to increase exponentially, and before long, we are even questioning the deepest parts of our being.

How could I have been so misled?

What went wrong in my plans?

How did I end up here?

What is wrong with me?

And the worst one: who even am I?

Sometimes in life, our gaze is so focused on our dreams that along the way, we lose sight of the man or woman who decided to begin the journey of the dream in the first place. We become so invested that we will do whatever it takes to win the prize, get to the finish line, and complete the mission we have set for ourselves. Somewhere along the way we forget who we were at the beginning. Our dreams haven't changed, but the person chasing them has.

It's been one year and seven months since I wrote this chapter. One year and seven months ago I had an inkling to write this book but had no idea what it would turn into. Here I am today, scrapping 90 percent of this chapter and starting over. I had no idea back then how much I would change and what all I would soon discover that would be worth sharing with you – all I knew was that I had *something* that needed to be shared. Now upon returning, upon finishing the rest of this book, it's remarkable to see the journey I went on and the key pieces that helped me change trajectory and inwardly transform into a version of myself I can confidently say is so much closer to the person I was created to be.

Sometimes it takes following your gut first and figuring out the rest of the details along the way.

You may not know now what it is that is hindering you from stepping into the person you are destined to be, all you know in your gut is that you have untapped potential, and you are eager (or maybe hesitant) to learn more. You have a flicker of desire set inside of you telling you that there's more out there and there's certainly more in you. You may have recently had your world turned upside-down and realized, as I did, this is the perfect time to start from the ground up. Or you may be wanting to pack your arsenal before you get to the next battle.

Either way, I cannot give you the perfect formula of what it looks like to journey through introspection and come out on the other side totally transformed; there isn't a one size fits all. But what I can give you is my experience and what I found on my quest for truth in hopes that it further guides you and directs you on your own quest. My hope is that when you get stuck and aren't sure where to turn, you can go back to messages in this book and use them as a slight nudge to get back on the right path. In the beginning, I had no idea what I was looking for, but I knew I was looking for something. As I mentioned earlier, I had been chasing a dream I was sure about but lost clarity on who I was in the aftermath. Pivoting from that and moving forward, I wasn't sure exactly what I was chasing but I found *myself* through the process and became significantly more resolute in the aftermath.

As C.S. Lewis says, "We all find what we truly seek." Our subconscious can sometimes have a mind of its own and even though you may not know exactly what you are searching for, it's inevitable that you will find it if you continue onward. I went out looking for answers about God, about the world around me, about relationships, love, purpose, morality, understanding, and the interconnectedness of it all; what I found was not only some of that but a deeper version of myself who only came about because of this journey. I went looking for answers to everything but me yet found the best version of her along the way. She wasn't wholly discovered at the end destination but was slowly unveiled, layer upon layer, with each next quest for truth.

For you, I can only hope that this book beckons you into the world of self-discovery and from there your peaked sense of inquisitiveness bleeds into other avenues of your life. I hope you not only learn your shortcomings and choose to grow from them, but I hope you simultaneously, and maybe unintentionally, reveal beautiful parts of you that you never knew existed- parts of you too precious to be buried in the shallow sand. Parts of you that need more than a shovel to dig down and find. I hope you find a yearning for truth, no matter the cost, and realize that sometimes it's not all about the answers, but about the chiseling away of yourself to get to what's inside along the way.

The journey isn't easy, and there are many variables at play that will stump you, confuse you, and challenge you to think again. In the coming chapters we'll pull apart ways to analyze your behavior, your thoughts, your fears, your goals and dreams, your reactions, and the idea you have of yourself. We'll discuss the factors that have made you who you are, and the factors that are leading you to who you'll soon become without a direction change. We'll walk through questions posed to raise your self-awareness, talk about how that awareness leads to growth, how growth pushes us closer to being intentional with our lives, and lastly, how intentionality is the gatekeeper for what it takes to build our confidence.

As you read through these pages, you'll likely notice a change in tone, change in writing style, and an overall change in comfort as I write. Reading through this one last time, I'm stunned at how obvious the journey really was. The changes speak for themselves throughout my growth as a writer and as a person over the course of this book. Instead of going back to rewrite some of the early chapters, I want you to be able to see that increase in confidence, increase in vulnerability, and increase in the resoluteness of my voice from this chapter to the end. I hope as you read my words, you'll feel as if you have a friend walking alongside of you, trying to figure this thing out with you.

To wrap up this chapter, I want to give you some resources you may find useful digging into before we journey on.

Enneagram

Apologetics

Visual Art

I know at first glance these three things don't seem like they have anything in common, but I've come to realize that each one of them is a great starting place for self-awareness.

The Enneagram helps you find the truth about yourself.

Apologetics speaks the truth and demands you listen.

And visual art helps others see the truth within themselves.

Let me elaborate on each one a little further.

ENNEAGRAM

The Enneagram, in simple terms, is a nine-sided figure that depicts a spectrum of personality types. However, when I explain the Enneagram to people, I always say that it is not like a Myers-Briggs or a test to tell you if you are an introvert or extrovert. Those things don't give us any more insight than letting us know if we had the choice to go to a party or stay inside and read a book, which we would choose. For most of us, we would choose either depending on the day. The Enneagram is a test that dives into your subconscious to pull out the answers of not what we would choose in situations, but why we choose them. I once came across a quote that described the many other personality tests and said that they are basically showing us what we would decorate our houses like, from the wall color to the furniture to the wall-hangings. The Enneagram doesn't show us the decorations in the house, but rather the structure of the house—how the house is built.

The Enneagram shows us our biggest insecurities and what we can do to embrace them, learn from them, and push past them. It shows us our deepest fears and how those negatively affect our choices. It shows us what we can do with every quality we have and how we can become the healthiest versions of whichever of the nine personality types we are.

The Enneagram doesn't sugar-coat our weaknesses; it boasts about our wretched tendencies that have the power to destroy us and those around us if we let them. However, it also gives us a path of hope, and it outlines strategies that will give us the confidence to embrace who we are by being able to grow into the best version of ourselves. The Enneagram is a great place to start if you are looking to do some soul-searching and self-analysis but should truly only be used in the beginning; the rest of your journey should be gone at alone.

APOLOGETICS

I believe apologetics is a subject that everyone can learn something from, whether a follower of Jesus or not. Wes Mullins, one of my favorite apologists and a dear friend of mine wrote *Unabashedly Resolute*, an incredible introduction to apologetics. The entire first book in this series mentions nothing of Jesus Christ or God at all; he outlines the importance of being able to decipher truth in today's world. He speaks about our communicational interpretation with one another and how the truth cannot lie in the hands of the receiver; the truth lies in the hands of the sender. Truth is embedded in the intentionality of the person giving it. The person receiving has no control over what they receive, only how they react to receiving it. This is where our feelings and emotions come into play when trying to interpret the truth. I once wrote a post on social media that highlights this thought exactly:

We live in a society where feelings dominate our responses to situations. We say we want to believe in truth yet cling so tightly to our emotions that we let them determine whether we turn right or turn left. How naïve are we to believe that true guidance and direction is based on futile feelings that are more or less a result of our own subconscious conjuring, what/who we listen to and see every day, and frankly how we felt when we woke up that morning. Truth is found in the deep dark alley where feelings and emotions are unable to be seen. Truth is truth no matter how we choose to react to it.

One of the purposes of apologetics is to give people the tools to be able to find truth in their lives, to be able to distinguish the naked truth without it being covered up by emotions, feelings, and other spiritual highs.

VISUAL ART

I would not doubt that many of you reading this don't claim to be an artist or maybe not even an appreciator of art, but I hope after this I can make you believe the importance of having art in our lives.

Ever since I was a young girl, I have always loved art. I grew up an only child, and since I had no siblings to spend time with, my parents would often find me in my room painting and drawing. Sometimes they'd even find me outside hand-building bowls and cups out of red clay mud.

Fast forward to today, I am still creating visual art as much as I can. When coming to college at the University of Kentucky, I decided to add an art studio minor to my economics degree so that I could still be involved in something that brought so much joy to my life and gave me the creative outlet I needed, away from all of the data, statistics, and numbers. I started working in the metal shop on our campus and fell in love with sculpture. I learned the processes behind metal casting and fabrication, and I even learned some blacksmithing. From that, I gravitated towards clay and began creating small- and large-scale sculptures out of clay.

To this day, creating art is something that moves me unlike anything else. I have realized how important it is to have a healthy vice, something where we can take all of our emotions and thoughts and push them through an outlet to become something tangible. We tend to underestimate the power of a release, and whatever that thing is for you—do it!

The reason that I wanted to include art in this chapter isn't because I have a passion for it and believe everyone should. I have simply realized that art is so much more powerful than just a pretty painting on the wall in a hotel or a sculpture in the middle of a park. When we look at visual art, we have to realize that someone went through a journey while creating the piece. Someone was going through an emotional experience and let those feelings guide what they created. Art is the most vulnerable, and intimate form of any tangible object. Art speaks the raw truth behind the artist, whether we can comprehend it or not, whether we "get it" or not.

To better demonstrate what I mean, I once decided in college that I wanted to attempt a sculpture of a woman standing with her arms raised, almost as if in offering up to the sky. I wanted her to embody confidence and strength, but also surrender and grace. I wanted her to express freedom. I also wanted her not to have an identity; therefore, the piece is only from the waist up to the neck. I wanted every woman who looked at her to be able to relate to who she is and see themselves in her.

As I finished creating her, I realized that her figure was looking so much like mine. All of my artistic friends laughed and said, "That is how our subconscious works. We create things in our image, to reflect how we feel," and that's when it all clicked for me. I created this anonymous womanly figure, but deep down, she was me. I decided to title the sculpture "Liberated."

So fast forward once more. It had been over a year since I created and documented "Liberated." I was moving houses, from a college house to a big-girl apartment closer to my new job. Boxes were piled up in my living room, along with all of my art, but virtually nothing else was left in the house. It had been just a few hours since I received a call that changed what I thought my future would be, forever. I remember sitting alone in my house as the rain poured outside, and my eyes were releasing their own set of tears. I remember questioning everything I thought I knew, everything I was so sure of.

How could a strong, independent woman like me allow herself to feel this way?

I sat there for hours hearing nothing but the rain on the roof and the creaking of an empty house. I remember sitting on my knees on a broken-down cardboard box in the middle of my living room. The lights were all off except a string of lights hanging above the window, and I sat on my knees, head down, weeping.

When I finally had the strength to lift my head, I saw my sculpture standing in front of me. She was backlit from the lights hanging by the window, and she looked absolutely stunning.

She was glowing.

I looked at her and remembered the Katlyn that created her, that created her to be in my image and to embody the strength I once felt. I gazed at her and realized that she was still me. She was still the me deep beneath the hurt and the pain. So I began to raise my hands, just as she does.

To this day, that has been the most liberated I have ever felt.

The truth is not determined by our circumstances or how we feel. The truth is the truth, no matter what our emotions tell us. From that day forward, I have believed in the importance of finding the truth about ourselves at all costs because sometimes we are so misled about who we are that we fail to see our true selves beneath the baggage we are carrying at the moment.

We are all destined to feel liberated, destined to become fierce. It may just take some work to get there.

I THINK WE UNDERESTIMATE THE POWER OF TRIGGERS AND HOW IT TAKES A VERY LONG TIME TO DEFUSE SOMETHING THAT HAS CAUSED A FIRE IN OUR MINDS FOR SO LONG.

TAKE INVENTORY

Isn't it funny how naïve we can be when it comes to the things we believe every day? We will argue with someone all day about something we read about and believe wholeheartedly; meanwhile, the source we received our "news" from was a platform such as Twitter, Facebook, or maybe a highly credible website such as Wikipedia (insert sarcasm here). There is something in us that initially takes things as they are. We are a "guilty until proven innocent" society that believes the majority of the things we hear, and we are either too lazy to dig into the real truth, or we don't care enough but are likely to spout off what we read or heard to anyone we see that day without caring if we are giving them reliable information or not.

The same is true for how we treat ourselves. Either we are really great at believing what others say about us and deeming their opinions worthy and valid, or we listen to nothing anyone else says about us and believe what we choose to tell ourselves. We are so easily swayed either way, depending on the day, and most of the time, we are choosing the wrong voices to listen to on each subject.

This is why it is important to get to the root of the truth. Yes, you may tend to feel your blood pressure climb when someone calls you that one specific name or mentions that one specific word, but why? What is the source of it? Did you have someone previously in your life use that word towards you, and it has scarred you ever since? Does that word bring up a past that you always try to run from? We have triggers in our lives that are a result of something else, and if we ever want to get a grasp on them, we have to become more self-aware.

Are you not afraid of rejection but completely petrified of vulnerability, of letting someone know the things that hurt you? Are you the opposite? Are you okay with sharing the deepest parts of yourself with someone else but you shudder at the thought of someone not reciprocating your desire for a relationship? Does failure scare you, or does the risk of failure excite you? Do you want to please everyone around you, or are you typically a self-preservationist who always looks out for yourself first? Are you so competitive that you can never play a game "just for fun," or can you never take anything seriously because that means there's no expectation from others for you to succeed?

We should be asking ourselves these types of questions because who would want to be in a relationship with someone who is afraid to share how they truly feel? Who would want to be with someone who can never have fun because, for some reason, everything in their life is a competition? Who wants to be friends with someone who always goes with the flow and doesn't take anything too seriously because that is easier than setting goals for themselves and others seeing them fail? We are all unique and have these things called "uncontrollables" in our lives. They are innate traits built into us, but it is our job not to let those traits manifest into something that we don't desire for ourselves.

Someone who tends to be soft-spoken, quiet, and maybe even un-social can be an amazing leader, but they can also let their fears and what others say about them dictate whether they step out of their comfort zone. It's also easy for someone who is confident and an outspoken leader to let their natural tendencies take them down a road that causes them to become arrogant, demanding, and condescending to others. It is imperative to take inventory and learn not only what qualities are currently defining you but also how they came to define you in the first place.

OUR PAST EXPERIENCES

One of the biggest factors in why we are the way that we are today is our past experiences. I think we all have those oddly vivid memories from random moments in our childhood that either scarred us or were some of the happiest moments of our lives thus far. However, I believe the moments that truly shape us are those that we try to forget or that we have never even really come to terms with from the start. Those are the memories worth seeking out because they are the ones subconsciously controlling us more than we can imagine.

For example, it wasn't until I was a senior in college that I realized why I had such a bad reaction to alcohol. I always told people, "Alcohol just isn't for me," but I never took the time to realize why it bothered me so much. I remember a time when I was with a group of friends, and one of them that I cared about deeply had a drink. I remember smelling the alcohol on their breath, and immediately my hands began to shake, my heart began to race, and I thought I was going to be sick. It was just one drink; what was the big deal? It wasn't until then that I began to realize that it wasn't just something I didn't like. It was a trigger for me. When I saw someone I cared about with it, I went into this crazy state of mind that I couldn't control. From that day on, I began to reflect and think back to my experiences with alcohol, and I wanted to know why something so silly had such a strong hold on me. After some time, I started recalling many memories from a very young age up until high school that revolved around alcohol ruining many things for the people I loved, and ultimately hurting me in the process.

To this day, I don't know if it was one experience that caused this or if it was many of them combined.

It could have been my grandfather that was an alcoholic for many years of my childhood.

It could have been the time I remember leaving a concert when I was little, and a family friend had one too many drinks and tried to fistfight every person they saw while we were walking to the car.

It could have been the anger I have seen in a family member when they drink too much. It could have been the time when I was in high school, and the boy I had been dating for years cheated on me, and his excuse was that he had been drinking.

It could have been how I have been sober at many parties and seeing how little control people have with what they say and do and how that scares me.

Vulnerability scares me, and alcohol brings that out in everyone.

It could be one of these things, or it could be a few of them, but either way, I found clarity. I realized how I am letting the past affect the way I see today, and whether I choose to drink or not is a choice I get to make, but it isn't fair for me to feel this way every time someone I love chooses to drink. I think we underestimate the power of triggers and how it takes a very long time to defuse something that has caused a fire in our minds for so long. It takes patience, and it takes love. It takes realizing things about yourself that you don't like and taking small changes to alter the way you think, and sometimes they still come back up and take control.

An article from *Good Therapy* explains a theory behind how triggers work: "One of the functions neglected during a fight or flight situation is short-term memory formation. In some cases, a person's brain may misfile the traumatic event in its memory storage. Rather than being stored as a past event, the situation is labeled as a still-present threat. When a person is reminded of the trauma, their body acts as if the event is happening, returning to fight or flight mode." Although the psychology behind how we process information like this is hard to control, the important thing is to make yourself aware.

Awareness is power, and the more aware we become of why certain things bring out emotions in us the way they do, the better we will be able to handle them. This is also an important time to say: love the people who have things that cause their hearts to beat quicker and their hands to tremor. Whether you realize it yet or not, we all have different things in our lives that set us off, make us upset, cause us to doubt or be fearful. We all have insecurities for different reasons. You aren't always going to understand why someone reacts the way they do, and sometimes you never will understand, but love them anyway. Choose them anyway, and in those moments, choose to be selfless and remember that something caused it for them. Life isn't about stopping everything you do in order to make others happy, but true happiness is only true happiness if it's something that makes those we love and care about happy too.

Choose to sacrifice for someone.

Choose to be patient with them.

Choose to have grace, and ultimately choose to love them for who they are.

No matter what that means for you.

RESULT OF OUR ENVIRONMENT

The second factor is our environment. A quote that I have tried to live my life by is from Jim Rohn, who says, "You are an average of the five people you spend the most time with." This quote has stuck with me over the years, and I am constantly evaluating what voices I am letting speak into my life. I think we tend to listen to far too much because we don't realize the impact words can make on our lives. The "in one ear and out the other" logic is not plausible to us humans.

Words stick with us, and if they don't stick in our conscious mind, they stick in our subconscious. Our actions and choices are guided by the congregation of thoughts, beliefs, and words we have taken in from others. The things we see every day, along with the people we interact with, have a significant impact on who we are at this very moment.

I always laugh at how we Americans tend to live in our own little bubble of the world. We get more excited about college football, a sport only us Americans play, than we do when Team USA is competing in the Olympics against countries from around the world. Most of us would typically be fine with a trip to Florida every year instead of saving up for a trip to Europe or Australia or Africa. We can easily be labeled as the epitome of ethnocentrism, and even though I also am beyond proud to be an American and will always shed a few tears when the National Anthem is played, we do tend to live in a fantasy world that isn't concerned with anything outside of our scope of these fifty states, or even our own state for some people.

The issue doesn't lie in being happy where you are; the issue lies in not being open-minded to understanding that there is more out there than what we know, understanding that our way isn't always the right way, and it certainly isn't the only way. We get so used to seeing the same things, talking about the same things, and living our daily lives as if there is nothing better out there that we start to take repetition as a synonym for truth. Just because something is common doesn't mean it is normal. If we listen to the same things every day, eventually, we start to believe it no matter how crazy it might be.

I remember in college, one of my best friends was from California, and we would always argue whether the thing you push around in a grocery store is called a "buggy" or a "cart." I, from the

South, would always call it a buggy, and she would always call it a cart. My argument was that a cart was a golf cart, and she argued that a buggy was a horse and buggy from the eighteenth century. One day, my friend from South Africa listened to the argument, and I could see how perplexed he was by all of this. Finally, he looked at us and said, "Are you guys talking about a trolley?" To this day, I still laugh at that moment and think about how so many of our opinions and beliefs are based on the environments we are in.

I am a strong believer in being proud of where you came from, proud of where you are, and proud of where you are going, but we can't fall into the trap of believing that where we have been, where we are, and where we are going are the sole definitions of truth. We have to keep searching, questioning, and evaluating how our environments shape us, what they are making us believe, and how they are guiding our choices every day.

YOUR POTENTIAL IS
LIMITED TO THE AMOUNT
OF HUMILITY YOU ALLOW
YOURSELF TO FEEL.

UGLY TRUTH

In every good book, every good movie, there is a part that no one wants to see. There is always that sad period where you feel so empathetic for the characters, for the good guys. Something terrible happens, and it looks like the story is broken beyond repair. Then all of a sudden, a superhero comes to save the day, the brokenhearted girl finds the new man of her dreams, Simba comes back to save the Pride Land, Harry defeats Voldemort, and Alfred Borden gets final revenge on Mr. Angier. (If you didn't get any of the references, you should google them and watch those movies ASAP). This chapter is one of those moments before the crowd cheers, applauds, and cries happy tears.

This is one of those chapters that try to show you the bad before you can see the good. It's sad how we humans can never truly appreciate things for what they are. It is almost as if we have to have something tragic happen before we ever really understand the value of anything. That in itself should show how broken of a people we are in desperate need of some work.

We always hear people talk about the "ugly truth," the truth that no one wants to hear but needs to hear it. Here's my version of the ugly truth: Your potential is limited to the amount of humility you allow yourself to feel. Read that again. How do we expect to teach a person something who already believes they know it all? And I think it's also very easy to say the opposite, to pity ourselves and say that we know nothing, but pity and humility are far from the same thing.

Pity is attention-seeking.

Humility is an authentic feeling of knowing one is less than, one has room for improvement, and one admires those above them in specific areas. It comes from a place of integrity not cowardice.

Pity is about feeling bad for yourself for not being adequate and wanting others to feel bad for you too. Dr. Maurice Nicoll says in one of his books, *Psychological Commentaries on the Teaching of Gurdjieff and Ouspensky*, "When a man pities himself, he feels he is owed—like the dog. If you feel that you are owed, you will never begin truly to work on yourself."

If we sincerely have a desire to grow, to reach our potential in every aspect of life, but primarily focusing on our character, we have to surrender this prideful, egotistic way of life that we all take part in. Some of us may struggle with it worse than others. Still, we all have times that we use the defense mechanism of pride to protect our feelings, to harden our hearts, and to convince others of a false confidence so that everyone knows we are capable and not helpless. In reality, none of this is true. In reality, none of us are perfect enough for each other. I am not a good enough friend, student, employee, daughter; the list goes on and on. I am not perfect at any of those things, and frankly, I don't believe I am even good enough to be speaking these words right now, but that is the point.

We can never truly reach our potential until we become more willing to listen to the ugly truth about who we are, what we struggle with, where we need improvement, and how sometimes we are unlovable because of selfish tendencies that have become too habitual and comfortable for us ever to notice or change. Sometimes we are too in our own head, reaffirming what we already know and convincing ourselves that the way we handle situations is the right way. We are too blind to see how wrong we truly are.

Nicoll also says in his book *The New Man*, "Truth must enter and grow in a man before he can change the direction of his will— that is before his feeling of what is good can change." In other words, we will always reaffirm our beliefs of what we think is good as long as what we believe is true doesn't change. If we believe that waffles cause cancer, we will probably do everything in our power not to let the ones we love and care about eat waffles. What we believe is good or bad is solely based on what we believe to be true. Until we learn to change what we believe is true, our actions will never truly change. That's because what we believe is good has not changed. If I finally learn that waffles do not cause cancer, that what I believed to have been true was actually false, only then will my actions change and my belief of what is good and bad change; I'll probably race to Waffle House that day.

We have to become open to learning more about ourselves and stop reaffirming our beliefs simply because they are *our* beliefs. Circular reasoning is a trap that always seems to be disguised as validated truth to the person speaking and believing it.

TRANSPARENCY

During my senior year of college, I led a group of about twelve freshman girls in a Bible study every week. We would spend time together talking about scripture and how their weeks went. A lot of the time, they would ask for advice or guidance on different situations in their lives. I remember when I interviewed to be a leader for this type of group, I thought to myself how awesome it would be to be a mentor to girls starting their first year of college. I thought about how intense my first year was and how pivotal those first few months were in shaping me and guiding me into the woman I became throughout the rest of my college career. You gravitate towards different hobbies, friend groups, and organizations and truly find your niche during your first year of college. Looking back, every year was a new adventure, and I met more people, got involved in new things, and dropped old things, but my freshman year still set the pace for my goals, dreams, and even the culture of people I wanted to spend my time with.

Being a mentor for young women going through that phase of life was a big responsibility for me, and I remember thinking about how important my influence would be on them, whether I liked it or not. I would be someone that spoke advice and direction into their lives, so I needed to make sure I was in the proper place myself to do so. The first week came around, and I decided to open the conversation with values that I wanted our group to live by. To this day, I remember telling them, "This is going to be a group of complete transparency. I want you all to know that I am going to be 100 percent open and honest with anything you ask me and anything you desire to know." I proceeded to tell them how none of us would truly grow from the group if we were too scared to ask difficult questions or, more importantly, if we were too scared to get difficult answers.

I have been in plenty of groups in my life that have felt not only awkward but also cold and sterile. I never wanted my group to be a group of weird moments of silence and clean conversations that are just covering up dirty, messy topics that are at the root of our problems. And isn't it funny how that is how we are in our own personal lives as well? We love to have these well-put-together moments of clarity with ourselves. We might even address an issue that we have or come to a realization that we might need to alter some behavior in our lives, but rarely do we ever come completely clean with ourselves. Rarely do we ever come completely clean with the people around us that we supposedly trust.

We are constantly trying to admit our problems by wrapping a big bow around them when we discuss them with others so that it doesn't seem as bad as it truly is. We are okay with others knowing we have issues but not issues that are too big to fix or too messy to discuss. We would never want others to think that we are too broken to be fixed or cause anyone to feel uncomfortable with our shortcomings and problems. We would never want our friends to think that we don't have it all together, or at least most of it together. To let them know you have the guilty pleasure of watching movies like *50 Shades of Grey*? Sure. To let them know that you struggle with an addiction to pornography? Never. To let them know that sometimes you struggle with jealousy and comparing yourself to others? Sure. To let them know that you have a tendency to talk bad about your friends or acquaintances when they aren't around to make yourself seem better to other people? Never. To get on the path of learning genuine, raw self-awareness, we have to be willing to not only acknowledge the ugly truth about ourselves but also be transparent enough to verbalize it to those who can help—to the people who truly love us.

Later on, we will discuss the importance of community and how only forming ideas and opinions about yourself, from yourself, is a dangerous place to be. We need to be not only transparent with ourselves but also transparent to those who love and care for us enough to help us see through the blinders we have been wearing for so long.

Transparency is hard, but once you master it, you will learn that the liberation you feel from being completely unhidden from your flaws is worth it.

VULNERABILITY

The only thing harder than transparency is vulnerability. Transparency is showing the honesty and complete clearness of the problem, while vulnerability is being willing to express the problem to begin with. It is challenging for some of us to open up and let someone into our life's struggles and issues.

If you have yet to do any research on the Enneagram, here is another chance for you to do so. I can tell you that I am a Type 8, also referred to as the "Challenger." And the biggest fear of a Type 8 is vulnerability. We 8's are typically assertive, courageous, independent, and thrive in leadership positions where we get to make decisions and have the responsibility to carry the rest of the team. We are deeply passionate, and the people we care about mean the world to us. We are protective and believe in taking up for those we love. We are an all-in or all-out kind of people. A competitive and "go big or go home" kind of people. You'll learn if you dive into understanding the Enneagram, or if you are already an Enneagram connoisseur, that every type has their strengths and weaknesses—areas they are naturally great at and areas that need some work (for some reason I feel like us 8's always need the most work). You'll learn not what you do but why you do it. You'll learn what deep fears and insecurities cause you to react to things the way that you do. You'll learn how you process information and how you communicate it out to others.

The Enneagram has exposed to me a great deal about who I am, but it has also helped me discover so much about who I am not. I am not the type to let things go without being confronted. I am not the type to tell you my entire life story when I first meet you or maybe even after I've known you for months or years. I'm not the type to be physically affectionate to others. I'm not the type to naturally call up my friends when something goes wrong in my life. I bottle things up. I investigate situations on my own. I am afraid of not being strong enough when someone needs me, not being independent enough when someone leaves, but most of all, I tend to be terrified of vulnerability.

Terrified.

All of these fears and insecurities I have can be summed up

or traced back to vulnerability. And the irony of that is so great because people like me hate admitting that something scares them. Letting people know that vulnerability is something we are scared of is a moment of vulnerability within itself.

The moment we see it coming, we run as fast and far away as possible.

The moment we feel the pull from someone to be vulnerable, to open up, to share something deep within us, we retreat.

The moment we feel someone trying to poke and pry in our lives, the moment we feel someone is trying to break down the walls we have worked so hard to put up, we run.

How cowardly, right? I live my life with such an attitude of fierceness; how could I allow something like this to cause me to raise my white flag, to surrender?

Whether you are a lion or a sheep, whether you admit your fears openly or keep them closed up so tightly, whether you have countless fears or just a few, we all have areas in our lives that cause us to tremble. We all have baggage that needs to be picked up and carried every day, and what I have learned is that those who are brave enough to let others in, let others see their failures, their insecurities, their fears, those are the fiercest and bravest people I have ever known. Those are the people in control of their lives, who have the most confident grasp on who they are, who understand that true strength comes from understanding and combating your weakness, not hiding it.

Vulnerability isn't telling everyone you meet what areas you need to improve or telling them things that scare you. Vulnerability is seeing someone willing to encourage you, challenge you, inspire you, and lift you up. It is choosing to let them in because you know by doing so you are:

1. Conquering your fears
2. Allowing someone else to help you become more self-aware and grow.

Our fears can only control us if we bury them beneath the surface, because buried things that are not tended to start to grow. They slowly sprout without our noticing, and they eventually become an untamed garden that we cannot control. Rip up your fear of vulnerability by the roots and believe that what was once your weakness has now become your strength. Have enough humility to expose the most vulnerable and tarnished parts of yourself so that you can begin to work in your garden, and someone else can begin to help you.

The ugly truth has to be acknowledged and managed before the pretty truth can ever be revealed and appreciated.

THE SOONER YOU TAKE
CONTROL OF REALIZING
WHO YOU ARE, THE SOONER
THOSE THINGS WILL NO
LONGER HAVE THE POWER
TO TELL YOU WHO YOU WILL
ALWAYS BE.

PRETTY TRUTH

Now that the ugly truth is out of the way, let's focus on the pretty truth. People always love getting the bad news before the good news. It seems that ending on a high note leaves us all in a much better place than ending on a low note—even if sometimes the bad news packs a heavier punch than the good.

I remember being in college and learning about the power of endings. Since then, I have reluctantly been reminded of it even more, but the start of this was in one of my economics classes as an upperclassman at the University of Kentucky. We talked about behavioral economics and how a study reflected that humans highly favor losing first and then winning rather than vice versa. I don't remember all of the details, but the study referred to two different groups of people and how one group would have $100 taken away from them, and then later on that day, they would somehow win it back. The other group of people would win $100 at the start of the day later to only have it lost in some way or taken back. I remember being so surprised at the significance of how many participants at the end of the study were much happier overall if they first lost the money and then gained it back. We talked about this study for a while and how there are many ways we can be deceived by the order of circumstances in our lives.

Then, just a few months ago, I found a note typed in my phone from a podcast or sermon I listened to that spoke on this exact thing as well. It referred to another observational study that dealt with two different patients in a hospital. One was experiencing extreme amounts of pain for a much longer time throughout the day, but their pain slowly eased up towards the end of the day with the proper medicine. The other patient was in much less pain throughout the entire day but had a spike in pain at the end of the day right before being released. The first patient said it wasn't too bad, and the second patient said it was unbearable. All the while, the person observing both of these cases knew that the pain the first patient dealt with was undoubtedly worse than the second, but the second had a much worse ending, so that is what they based their experience off of.

The last example is a story of how a man went to hear a symphony performance at a theater. The entire performance was absolutely beautiful, but at the very end, someone hit the wrong note. It released a loud screeching sound just before the show concluded. The man who went to the show left feeling disappointed because the ending took the spotlight and everything before was only a forgotten memory.

I say all of this to tell you that endings are important. People might forget the details in the middle, or how everything began, but they will not forget the ending, good or bad. So even though the ugly truth is that we all need some work. We all need to step out of our comfort zones to become more vulnerable and transparent, and to experience humility; we also have encouragement that this is not the end. Where you have been and where you are now do not have to determine where you are going. The first step is feeling the humility of knowing that there is work to be done; the next is taking a step out in confidence, knowing that you are ready to better yourself and put in the work to become the person you are destined to be.

TAKE ACTION

Now that you know the importance of realizing your areas of improvement, of humility, of being vulnerable and letting others in, and of transparency with both yourself and others, take a moment to write down what you want to change.

Write down the parts of yourself that you are not proud of.

Write down ways you wish you could react differently.

Write down triggers that you don't want to be in control of your life anymore.

Write down your biggest fears, your smallest fears, and your irrational fears.

Write down those things that you hate admitting to yourself that you struggle with.

And finally, make a plan to combat those things. The problem with most of us is that we might get past the first step of recognition, but then we are too cowardly to take steps to change anything. There will be many things that you will know you want to change.

Maybe you have a bad temper.

Maybe you tend to speak condescendingly to others because

your achievements and success have given you a sense of entitlement.

Maybe you tend to get jealous.

Maybe you are trapped by countless tiny insecurities that collectively make you doubt your value.

Maybe you speak more than you listen to others.

Maybe you listen and struggle with opening up to those who want to help you, who want to encourage you.

Maybe you are just too comfortable, and change terrifies you.

Maybe you're afraid of rejection, so not taking the step of courage is easier than getting let down and rejected by someone.

Maybe you are missing out on the next big journey of your life because you are so terrified that the next thing won't live up to what you expect or that the next season of life will be challenging, so you would rather stay where you are.

Maybe you need a career change, a relationship change, a location change, but you are too scared to make the first move because staying is less work than leaving.

Whatever those things are, whatever grips you that you believe is hindering you from growing into the person you are supposed to be, write those things down. Then make small, intentional adjustments that will prepare you for the big switch you need to make. Every day when you wake up, read those areas that you aren't proud of and let the power of self-awareness consume you. The sooner you take control of realizing who you are, the sooner those things will no longer have the power to tell you who you will always be.

The pretty truth is that every one of us has what it takes to change. We have the will-power, the courage, the fierceness, the drive; we just have to let those characteristics overshadow the size of our fear. I see so many people doubting, questioning, and shrinking back when they have to face a moment of true vulnerability within themselves or with others. I want to know myself so well that there is nothing anyone else can tell me that I don't already know. I want to have my small group of encouragers, challengers, and inspirers that help me see my life from an outsider's perspective and fully realize my potential.

I don't want to live in denial of who I am, nor do I want to think I am better or worse than I am. I want to live in the reality of seeing all of the pretty and all of the ugly truth about myself so that I can take the steps to become more of who I was destined to be, and the fact is that I can't do all of that alone.

A big family I spent a lot of time with during my college years all have tattoos of teepees somewhere on their body; everyone in the family has one. When you ask them what it means, they all reply the same: "Find your tribe and love them fiercely." Something I want to challenge you with is seeking advice from others who know you the absolute best. This is a daunting task and goes back to the importance of taking into consideration the voices you are allowing to speak into your life every day. However, we are not made to do this life alone. We are created for relationships, friendships, and community.

If you don't have a strong community in your life, I encourage you to find them. It doesn't matter if it's only a couple of people or ten people. We all need other influences in our lives to help us spot the areas we can't see, the areas we are so zoomed into that we can't see the full picture. Even for someone like me, who thrives on independence, I have been reminded recently of the importance of community—of finding my tribe.

Growing up an only child nurtured me into the mindset of not needing anyone else to play games with. That evolved into not needing anyone to tell secrets to. That evolved into not needing anyone to comfort me when I am going through pain and adversity in my life. That evolved into me building up walls to keep others out so that I can handle this life on my own without others coming in just to leave me more disappointed. I was so afraid of opening up, because I had always been used to keeping it in. Then I learned that I had been living my life without something so important, so essential to experiencing confidence, freedom, and true love.

Of course I have always had my friends, but having friends and having people who will walk through the storms of life with you, having those who will pick up their swords and go to battle with you, that is something invaluable. I needed that, and I am so happy to say I have found it. These people are from so many different walks of life, most of them don't even know each other, but they all know me. They each individually have invested so much into my life. They have seen me at my best, my worst, and, most importantly, during seasons of pruning in my life. They have seen me in such deep anguish trying to figure out what parts of my life need to be trimmed, groomed, or maybe even stripped away. I will forever be thankful for those who will tell me the ugly truth and the pretty truth about myself.

A few days ago, I was with a couple of my friends sitting outside at a burger restaurant, just talking and enjoying the last few weeks of summer. If you know me, the "burger restaurant" part probably threw you off a little bit because it is definitely a rarity that I eat a burger. I am not a vegetarian, but burgers have just never really been my thing. So I was sitting there eating my burger and laughing to myself as I said, "It's definitely true that we question who we are when we go through the troubles of life. What's next, I dye my hair and go get a tattoo?" My friends just smiled and laughed and assured me that seasons are just seasons and sometimes it's good to get out of your comfort zone, sometimes the adversity life throws at us gives us the extra push we need to try new things and explore more. That advice alone was uplifting to me, and I remember just smiling back and embracing that truth as I ate a few more fries and dipped my burger into some ketchup (something else I never eat).

Being around friends is so nice, I thought. Being around people who will stop whatever they are doing to spend time with you because they know you are going through something rough is extra nice. We sat there in silence for a while and just enjoyed each other's presence, watching everyone around us and breathing in the warm summer air. Lately, I've just been happy being around people that love me. Just knowing someone is there has been so comforting for me lately, even if we don't say much.

Moments passed by, and I was almost finished with my burger when my friend looked at me and said, "Katlyn, what makes you happy?" It caught me so off guard, but if you know him and the relationship we have, you know it is not unusual for him to ask me a question like this. I sat there, a little scared but a little excited at the same time to answer. I asked him to elaborate because there are plenty of big things and small things, but he wouldn't.

What did make me happy?

This story's point isn't to tell you what makes me happy or how the entire conversation played out. The point is to tell you the importance of having friends who ask you questions like that. I had been so consumed in my own thoughts, wrapped up in a situation that I couldn't seem to find my way out of, and that moment I remember feeling an instant burst of joy and excitement. I was finally *made* to talk and think about something else, something that made me *happy*. I have always been thankful for our friendship, but at that moment, I was more grateful than ever before. A question so simple was so hard for me to answer because all that I had thought about for weeks was something that wasn't making me happy, the storm of life I was battling my way through. Gosh, how awesome was it to talk about the things that made me happy, if even for a moment. How awesome was it to have someone want to hear about my passions, the things that bring me joy. How awesome was it to have someone remind me of those things that I had forgotten about.

The conversation continued, and I finally responded with a few things. I talked about how concerts and music made me happy, how art made me happy, how one-on-one conversations made me happy, and lastly, what we were stuck on for the longest, was how "honesty" made me happy. We talked for a long time about the deep-rooted things that make me happy and how honesty is one of those. I cling to honest people, sometimes even the most blatant and brutally honest people. There is something in them that I deeply admire, even if what comes out of their mouths might be considered rude or unwarranted. I appreciate the confidence in those who are unafraid to speak the truth regardless of the repercussions it may have because they know the ugly truth is better than a pretty lie.

It was an awesome conversation that night, just as our usual ones are, but I will never forget the instant joy of having someone else force my thoughts to revolve around something good. I will never forget how those conversations are sometimes challenging but are always coming from a good place. I leave conversations like those knowing more about who I am and knowing more about what others have observed about me. I need to spend more time talking to people and listening to their perspectives on who they see me as or what my actions portray, and you should too.

There is an old Chinese proverb that says, "If you don't change your direction, you'll end up exactly where you're going." To some of us, that can be a scary place. So choose today to change your direction in whatever area of life you might need to change, in whatever fear it is that keeps you so tied down and consumed.

The pretty truth is that where we are now is not where we have to end up, but we have to take the uncomfortable steps now to recognize and pursue the changes we want to make. We have to acknowledge the truth and take hold of who we are now to experience true freedom in the future.

The pretty truth is that we don't have to go at this alone, and we aren't supposed to. Grab coffee with a friend or meet them for lunch.

Ask them how they perceive you, ask them what they think you are fearful of, what they see you run from.

Ask them what they think your dreams and passions are based on where you invest your time.

Ask them what they think are the most important priorities in your life just by observing you from the outside.

Ask them what they believe you can do to transform into a better version of yourself.

And then, make sure you listen.

Whether what is said is good, bad, pretty, or ugly, listen. This could be the restart and the fresh perspective you have needed for a long time.

WE FALL INTO DROUGHTS OF
SELF-PITY BECAUSE IT FEELS
BETTER TO PITY OURSELVES FOR
THE MISFORTUNES WE FACE THAN
TO CONFIDENTLY STAND UP TO
THOSE MISFORTUNES WITHOUT
LETTING THEM DEEPLY AFFECT
OUR INNER PEACE.

THE UNCONTROLLABLES

When I began thinking about this chapter, many different types of "uncontrollables" came to mind, so I decided to spend time on each one of them.

The Uncontrollables:

Around You
Within Yourself
Within Others

If you want this entire chapter to be summed up in one sentence, it would be this: Learn to recognize the uncontrollable elements in your life, within yourself, and within others, but stop allowing those things to have a louder voice in your life than the things you can control.

This world we live in is full of surprises. Think back to a time where within hours, your life was flipped upside down. We begin a day full of happiness and end a day full of tears. We begin a day sad and end a day with excitement about the future. Within moments our lives can be completely disrupted by the good or bad news we have no control over.

As I type this, I can't help but think of the significance of today. The date is September 11, and I am currently on a plane flying to the west coast. It's been nineteen years now since the attack on 9/11, but this uneasy ambiance still fills the air. The "Never Forget" posts cover social media, songs like "Proud to Be An American," "Courtesy of the Red, White, & Blue," and "Where Were You When the World Stopped Turning" are streamed today more than any other day of the year. If you're quiet enough you can hear the hushed whispers around the airport of people talking about how it still seems unsettling to be at an airport on a day like today.

Thousands of people went to sleep on September 10, 2001, with no idea that it would be their last night here on earth. So many innocent people had their lives ripped from them by the evil motives of someone else. There are many times like this that we start to question life in itself. We question how a good God can let things like this happen, and we tend to forget that we live in such a broken world that will never be perfect. Perfection will only be found for us on the other side of heaven because the Enemy "walks around, stalking his prey, and waiting for someone to devour."

Why would we need a God?

Why would we need heaven if everything always went as planned here on Earth?

Why would we need a savior, someone to lead us and guide us?

I am not nearly as credible as some of my favorite apologists when it comes to answering this question, but I do know the answers that have been brought to light to me through insight, research, and scripture. If we knew the true answers to questions like these, we would be God Himself, so the best we can do is see God's character, understand His plan by reading His Word, and deduce down our egos enough to understand that we will never know all of the answers. The bottom line is that we are all broken people; not one of us is "good." We all have selfish desires. We all struggle with acceptance, wanting to be loved at whatever the cost, and most of us struggle with pride. So bad things don't happen to "good" people. Bad things happen to all of us broken people.

The real question isn't "Why are these things happening?" Rather, it is "What am I going to do about it? How am I going to react to it? How will I make a difference in this fallen world until I reach the other side where there will be no tears, no sorrow, no death, no disappointment, no unpredictable, and no uncontrollable?"

AROUND YOU

I think we all have heard of the word stoicism or at least have heard of someone who was referred to as being "stoic." However, it wasn't until about a month ago that a friend of mine told me that I should look into the teachings of stoicism and start applying them to my life. I remember looking at him funny because I knew what stoicism meant, but as someone who loves research and loves to learn about different philosophies and theologies, I had never taken the time to dig into this subject.

So I recently began to do a more in-depth study on the principles and teachings of "stoicism," and without boring you to death on the history behind it, a short synopsis and the simplest definition

I have found so far comes from an article from *The Daily Stoic*:

> Stoicism has just a few central teachings. It sets out to
> remind us of how unpredictable the world can be. How
> brief our moment of life is. How to be steadfast and
> strong and in control of yourself. And finally, the source
> of our dissatisfaction lies in our impulsive dependency
> on our reflexive senses rather than logic.

As I read more about stoicism, I began to smile and think how perfectly this fits in with the ideology one needs to live a fierce life and what perfect timing it was for me to find this right before writing this chapter.

There are so many uncontrollable, unexpected, and unpredictable moments in our lives, and yet we still choose to be surprised and distraught by each of them when they occur. We are shocked beyond belief that something we were so unprepared for happened to us again. We are baffled that a person can change so quickly, that they can so easily betray us, lie to us, and turn their backs on us. We shake our fists at God when life doesn't give us what we thought we deserved, what made sense in our tiny brains. We fall into droughts of self-pity because it feels better to pity ourselves for the misfortunes we face than to confidently stand up to those misfortunes without letting them deeply affect our inner peace.

Stoicism teaches us to live a life unmoved by neither the harsh realities of life nor the good and encouraging moments. Stoicism zooms out to see the big picture of life and takes the good with the bad, the weeping with the rejoicing, the depression with the liveliness, the anxious with the peaceful. It sees the big picture of life and realizes one cannot exist without the other.

As we will discuss in a later chapter, one cannot have deep joy without first experiencing deep sorrow. Instead of letting the uncontrollable aspects of the things happening around you dictate your mood, energy, drive, ambition, and ultimately your confidence in living this life, become someone who treats a hardship as worthy as a victory. As the famous philosopher Marcus Aurelius once said, "Choose not to be harmed, and you won't feel harmed. Don't feel harmed, and you haven't been."

Of course, one can argue that this is a lot easier said than done, but an exercise that the first stoics used to put this ideology in place was called "Turning the Obstacle Upside Down." The article from *The Daily Stoic* puts it well:

What they meant to do was make it impossible not to practice the art of philosophy. Because if you can properly turn a problem upside down, every "bad" becomes a new source of good. Suppose for a second that you are trying to help someone, and they respond by being surly or unwilling to cooperate. Instead of making your life more difficult, the exercise says, they're actually directing you towards new virtues; for example, patience or understanding. Or the death of someone close to you, a chance to show fortitude.

Marcus Aurelius described it like this: "The impediment to action advances action. What stands in the way becomes the way." What a liberating way to look at the things of this life. I want to challenge you to begin to look at the uncontrollable aspects of life, the things that happen around you, the hardships that are keeping you anchored, keeping you tied up, and keeping your sails closed; look at those things through a lens of opportunity. They are giving you the outlet that you need, the push you need, that you would have never given yourself if you had the chance.

Stop letting the uncontrollables have such a hold over you. They too are a blessing that just needs more time to be revealed to you. "What stands in the way becomes the way."

Life is going to happen whether we are ready or not.

Adversity and devastating times will happen whether we like it or not, so choose to build your own level of strength, forbearance, perseverance, and willpower so that you are still standing after everything else has come crashing down.

WITHIN YOURSELF

I cannot speak for everyone around this; I can only give my personal antidote of how I have learned to deal with the uncontrollable within myself. I remember when I was a freshman in high school, my dad and I always seemed to be arguing about something. Typically, it was silly things that normal teenagers argue with their dad about, but I remember this one time when we were arguing about some profound things. We began talking about religion and philosophy and started going back and forth on what we believed to be true and why. The debate escalated pretty quickly, and I don't even remember exactly what we were talking about, but I will never forget the last thing he said to me that made the argument come to a halt. I remember standing next to the washer and dryer on the first floor of our tiny log cabin house when he looked at me and said, "Katlyn, you can't change how you feel. About anything. You can know you should or shouldn't feel a certain way, but no matter how hard you try, you can't change the way you feel on the inside. And I can't change how I feel about this right now." After that, I remember just dropping my head and running up the stairs to my room.

I have thought about that conversation many, many times since then. Whenever I get upset over something or let my emotions completely entangle me, I think back to that conversation. I have dissected it and replayed it in my head many times, and I think I have finally come to realize its truths and incongruities. The truth of the matter is that yes, sometimes we cannot truly help how we feel about a certain situation or person. Sometimes we know we deserve better or worse, and yet our feelings somehow tell us otherwise. If we knew that the significant other who cheated on us wasn't good enough for us, if we knew that we deserved better than that or better than the abusive relationship we are in, wouldn't it be easy to move on and get over it?

Just because we know something to be fact doesn't always make our emotions any easier or less intense. Often, we linger in those horrific relationships or circumstances because we allow our emotions and how we feel about a situation to override the truth of the situation. Ben Shapiro explains it eloquently when he says, "Facts don't care about your feelings." Even when our theology doesn't match up with our feelings, we have to decide which one we are going to give more weight to. Which one are we going to follow, and which one will we make our decisions based upon? I can live the rest of my life as if I am worthless because I was made to feel no longer needed or important after a parent walked out or after a breakup or broken marriage. But that isn't the truth. I can be made to feel like I have no future because I didn't get the job I applied for or because I made choices in my younger years that led me down a path I never thought I would be on, but those thoughts are nothing more than built-up lies and easy ways out because we are too afraid to keep going and try again; those thoughts aren't the truth.

The same goes for God.

The way we feel about God isn't significant; it's just mere opinion. What matters is the truth about God, whatever that may be. C.S. Lewis says it best in *The Weight of Glory*: "I read in a periodical the other day that the fundamental thing is how we think of God. By God Himself, it is not! How God thinks of us is not only more important but infinitely more important."

Our opinions, and usually false opinions, can be changed with a little work. The more we search for truth, the more we base our lives not on the opinions we *think* but on the truths we *know*, the sooner we will be able to take hold of the uncontrollables in our lives. We all have opinions, but the weight we give those opinions matter. The weight we give our feelings versus the facts we know to be true matters.

You wouldn't want a doctor making decisions on a patient based on the volatility of the patient's emotions. You would want the doctor to decide to do surgery or treatment based on facts and his knowledge base around modern medicine, not whether the patient seems compliant or is kicking and screaming. Nor would you want the doctor to take the advice of a patient who doesn't know how to properly read the x-ray. Sometimes how we feel about something doesn't line up with the facts to be known about the situation, and it's because we are human.

The problem is that we allow personal anecdotes, emotions, and built-up insecurities to cast a shadow over the facts we know to be true. Our job isn't to force away our emotions or force away from the real stories or the worthy pain swaying our thought process. The goal is to recognize that with some work and a yearning to chase the truth, as long as our focus is on the facts and not our feelings, we can slowly begin to loosen the chains that our emotions have on us.

We can begin to control the uncontrollable moods that sweep us into dark places because we have the truth to fight back against them.

I may feel unworthy, but I am not unworthy.

I may feel like a failure, but I am not a failure.

I may feel like I don't have a purpose, but I just haven't discovered it yet. I feel like God is against me, but based on His actions, He is more with me than anyone else, even more than I am with myself.

Glenn Beck says, "We have to stop asking God to be on our

team and start telling Him that we are on His."

The good news about feelings is that they are fleeting. The good news about the truth is that it never changes.

WITHIN OTHERS

The reason I explained "Within Yourself" before "Within Others" is because I hope now you'll realize that every battle we fight within ourselves, someone else is also fighting.

We need to have a little grace for people.

The rash people, the aggressive people, the irrational people, all of the people that none of us would admit we are. They are all fighting battles within themselves, just like you are.

"Hurt people, hurt people."

I think one of the biggest problems of our era is that we have forgotten about grace. It's always time for justice, it's always time for people to "get what they deserve."

Bob Goff says, "Grace never seems fair until you need a little."

And remember, my personality type thrives on justice. I constantly struggle with forgiveness, letting go, and being okay with God's timing in justice. I have just learned that no matter what I think someone else deserves, I don't know their story, nor do I know the full story of the situation. I've learned that there will be plenty of times when I look like the villain in someone else's eyes and whether I am at fault or not, I will also want grace.

I don't watch *Grey's Anatomy*, but my roommate does. I was watching a single episode with her once, and Meredith Grey watched as someone had been run over by a huge fire truck (I hope I recall the details of the story correctly, or else the *Grey's* fans will come attacking). She stood there as a loved one of the injured person was called and came running onto the scene. The person kneeled and was sobbing while the injured person lay there pinned between the ground and the truck. The loved one was screaming and begging someone to do something. Meredith looked at her counterpart and said something along the lines of, "If we move that truck, he is going to die." She began to get emotional, and her presumed friend/work partner looked at her and basically told her that she would be the hero of the story some days. Other days, even though she truly still is the hero, she will look like the villain. She will look like the one who caused the worst to happen, didn't do enough, couldn't save the day, but all of that is part of the job. The days she is the hero are worth the days like today when she looks like she is abandoning him when in reality, she is just trying to give him a few more moments with someone he loves before he passes. She was trying to give the loved one just a few more moments with him.

I've thought about that story a lot. How often am I either the true villain or simply the one who looks like the villain in someone else's story? And how grateful am I for those who have given me grace and loved me through it anyways. Whether intentional or not, we aren't always going to be the hero, and most of the time, those situations are uncontrollable.

Choosing to look at others who hurt us directly or indirectly and giving them grace is the greatest and most freeing thing we can do. Justice will come when it's ready, but justice isn't our job to serve. We aren't nearly qualified enough, and we don't have anywhere close to a clear enough track record of our own.

Lay down the weapons we choose to bear to hurt others for the grievances they've caused us. Instead, pick up the weapons that we can use to win wars truly waged against us, the wars we *can* control and conquer ourselves.

PART II

Growth

WE HAVE TO START
PARTICIPATING IN THE
CONSTANT BATTLE OF LOSING
OUR ENTITLEMENT TO TRULY
BEGIN OUR JOURNEY OF
GROWTH.

ENTITLEMENT

Some would argue that one of the biggest problems with our world today is entitlement. Entitlement is so close to selfishness that sometimes the two can be mistaken for one another. Entitlement is defined in the Oxford dictionary as, "the fact of having a right to something or the belief that one is inherently deserving of privileges or special treatment." So when people are asked why they feel so entitled, the common response would be one of defensiveness and justification of the situation at hand. No one wants to admit that they feel entitled, much less admit that they are acting selfishly. However, every day, our greedy tendencies and self-preserving ways of life show that we always manage to feel entitled to receive what we *believe* we deserve.

The keyword there is what we "believe" we deserve.

The issue lies in the fact that we are all broken, imperfect, and egotistical people. Even the quietest and most introverted people still tend to feel the need to always have their needs met no matter the cost to someone else.

The difference in terms of Type A and Type B people is not that one is more demanding of their needs; it is that they react to their needs not being met in different ways. Both equally feel the emotional betrayal if they do not receive what, once again, they *believe* they deserve. If we were perfect, the righteousness behind entitlement would be completely justified. When we dig into this, we find the error is in believing that we are vindicated in our actions, thoughts, and beliefs, but others are not.

If I believe with everything in me that my ways are of truth, then anyone who believes otherwise is less than and deserves less than I do. In our culture we have become so obsessed with ourselves that we laugh at the idea that our ways are conditioned into us by how we grew up, the way we were treated, and the experiences we have had. We believe that all of our thoughts and beliefs are objectively chosen by us, conjured up by the unlimited wisdom and knowledge we have obtained. We think we have to be able to make the correct choice at all times, which has proven false time and time again.

One of the oldest discoveries about psychological conditioning comes from Ivan Pavlov, which many of you likely already learned about if you have ever taken an introductory psychology course. Pavlov noticed that his dog began to salivate not only when meat powder was present but also when the person consistently giving it to him was present. Pavlov continued researching this and discovered an extensive amount about how animals and us humans learn.

Our environments condition us based on punishments and reinforcements. When we choose one action and get either punished or reinforced by it, we remember this and subconsciously base our future actions around this. Conditioning isn't something that just happens overnight. Still, over time, we can become so accustomed to responding a certain way to situations that we don't take the time to realize why we are responding the way that we are.

Our outlook on life is constantly being changed by our experiences. As Stephen Covey said in his book *The 7 Habits of Highly Effective People*, "To change ourselves effectively, we first have to change our perception."

The birth of entitlement comes from believing that we are so confident in our ways that we know we deserve the utmost in every situation without considering the opportunity costs or other perceptions at hand. To begin to kill that deeply rooted feeling is to understand that our outlook on life is unique. It does not give us any more credit in this life than the next person's outlook does.

In later chapters, we will talk about the importance of credibility and how that leads to confidence, but credibility does not condescend or undermine others. Our credibility in some areas does not give us the authority to think less of others' needs and raise ourselves up on the totem pole of life.

So how does this play into growth?

When I was a young girl, I would always play "war" with my next-door neighbors. There were two boys my age and three younger girls. Each of us would get an airsoft gun and go into the woods behind our house right before sunset. We would decide teams and then break out and hide and when the time was right, we would run to find our opponent and obliterate them with as many airsoft pellets as we could. The problem was that we either never had enough guns, or when we did, one or two of them didn't work properly. So when it came time to split up into teams, the youngest girl would always get the gun that halfway did not work, or sometimes she would not get a gun at all—how ruthless, right? No matter how hard she tried, she was always on the losing team and always got shot one too many times, causing her to run inside crying after every round.

When I think about personal growth, there is no way around truly achieving it and coming out on the winning team without losing our sense of entitlement. If not, it is a helpless, losing battle every time. We can get up every morning and strive for personal growth. We can have the best weaponry out there. Still, without humbling ourselves and choosing to walk in vulnerability exposing our areas needing improvement, we will continue to get shot down every time. We will continue to believe that we deserve more than we truly do based on our personal assessment of our status and needs compared to others.

And when I say "lose our entitlement," I don't mean stripping down confidence or letting people walk all over you; I mean believing that you are a broken person needing redemption, needing some real work. It means understanding that you are not perfect and that others' shortcomings in your direction are not just okay but truly understood and taken with grace. As people, we will never be able to live up to others' expectations of us, just as they will not be able to live up to ours.

We have to start participating in the constant battle of losing our entitlement to truly begin our journey of growth.

GOD HAS TRULY BROUGHT ME
TO MY KNEES AND MADE ME
FACE THE HARSH REALITY THAT
WITHOUT PEOPLE TO GRIEVE WITH,
LOVE WITH, CELEBRATE WITH,
SUFFER WITH, WE CANNOT BE
THE STRONG WARRIORS WE WERE
CREATED TO BE.

TOUGH LOVE

A few chapters ago, we discussed the ugly truth and how important it is to understand those aspects of yourself. Now I want to explain how we can use those bits of self-awareness for growth. I explained how important vulnerability is and how we have to be willing to humble ourselves to those we trust so that we can get a clear view of who we are, one that isn't based on our own preconceived ideas of ourselves. However, who we let in is just as important.

I'm sure as a young adult you heard countless times that you needed to be careful of who you spent time with. I'm sure your parents, a teacher, or someone else told you how important it was to have good friends that don't lead you down the wrong path. Now, all of that is true, but what no one tells you when you grow up is how that statement is still true, and truer than ever. Maybe you aren't worried about your friends peer pressuring you now like you were when you were sixteen, but now you should be worried about your friends *not* pushing you into things you *should* be doing.

As I mentioned in the first section, Jim Rohn says, "You are the average of the five people you spend the most time with."

Take a moment and think about who those five people are.

Family? Friends? Colleagues? Or maybe no one. Maybe you can't even think of five people you spend time with.

Whether we like it or not, we were designed for community. I like to think that I can do anything and everything on my own, which is usually true; however, a person can only stand on their own two feet alone for so long. We were created to have fellowship with other humans.

Watch the television show *Alone* for a while, and you'll quickly learn how the human mind becomes desperate for human interaction after being alone in the wilderness for weeks and months at a time.

That said, the first people I want to address are those like me who think they can do life totally alone. I will also lump into this group the people who don't have many friends because they are content and not willing to find them, as well as those who desperately want them but haven't had any luck finding them. We all have to make a change.

For me, the issue is to stop being so prideful and rebellious, fending people off by putting up walls because of my fear of codependence.

For you, maybe you need to step out of your comfort zone and intentionally seek out community.

Find a Facebook group, join a group at church, join a club of some sort, spend time volunteering, start taking a new class on something you have always wanted to learn—do something to surround yourself with more people so that you can find community again. Maybe you have a fear of rejection or have been hurt by others too many times. Stop letting those fears take control of your life. I promise you, without community and people to inspire you, challenge you, encourage you, and simply to do life with you, you aren't living life in the abundance you could be.

Alone time is crucial, and I'll even discuss its importance in later chapters, but so is fellowship with like-minded people and un-like-minded people. I know others have likely hurt you and that is your excuse for keeping your walls up as it is for me. But as C.S. Lewis says, "There are far, far better things ahead than any we leave behind."

Give people a chance again. Stop selling others short because of the hurt from your past. Stop closing yourself off because you think they will end up treating you like someone else did. And stop losing faith that there are good people out there who would love you so deeply and want to walk through life with you. I promise you there are.

Believe again that the God who has intimately designed your story has the power to redeem your hurt and pain and give you the friend or partner you deserve or maybe don't deserve. Believe that He will show up and give you someone that will, as my friend told me, "give the 80 percent when you can only give 20 percent." We were never meant to carry it all. We were never meant to hold all of life's problems in our own hands. And when we selfishly choose to keep it all to ourselves, we typically crumble in defeat—not able to carry the weight of it all.

It's scary, it's uncomfortable, it's a lot of work, and it's a huge risk. But find your tribe and love them fiercely. Make an intentional effort to find them and to love them without hesitation, unconditionally.

Those of you who have your friends, close family, coworkers, or acquaintances (and maybe even plenty of them), be sure to choose them wisely. As tough as it is to realize, there are times in our lives when we need to go separate ways from some of the people we have been the closest to for many years. This isn't always the case, and lifelong friends are worthy of being cherished. However, more times than not, I've seen many people hang on to relationships and friendships just because they were content and comfortable in the situation. Just like anything else, we get comfortable and content with the people we share our lives with. We rarely take time to sit and ask ourselves about the relationship. We spend most of our time just living it and moving on with our lives. However, if we want to live out our days with intentionality and purpose, one of the first things we have to evaluate is our friendships and the people we spend the most time with.

Can you look at the people you spend the most time with and confidently say that they are making you better or pushing you closer to your ideal self?

Can you look at those five people that you are theoretically the average of and be happy with that?

Can you look at those five people and believe that you are on the right path to becoming better and reaching your potential because of them?

If not, it's time to reevaluate. If you don't have them at all, it's time to make an effort to find those people. They need you just as much as you need them.

One thing God has shown me over the last year and a half, and through the darkest days of my life thus far, is that I am not strong enough to do life on my own. As an only child, I felt like it was my nature to be independent, and honestly, I am still incredibly independent. However, I am not reluctant to believe that I *need* people, whereas I never used to admit that. God has truly brought me to my knees and made me face the harsh reality that without people to grieve with, love with, celebrate with, suffer with, we cannot be the strong warriors we were created to be. We are so much stronger together than we will ever be apart, and it has taken me years to admit that. But once again, the people we choose to be our strongholds matter.

The people we choose to go to war with matter.

My circle now is smaller than it has been my entire life, but it is more impactful than it has been my entire life. The people I allow to hear my cries, hear my celebrations, they are the ones who have called me out when I haven't been myself, pushed me to try things I would never have done on my own, and challenged me to dream bigger when I didn't believe in myself enough to do so.

Part of the reason I am even writing this book is that I have people who have believed in me and pushed me to do something so daunting and terrifying. I attribute the extra push I needed to apply for a promotion at work not too long ago to "my people." The joy I received when I bought my car not too long ago, the celebrations far exceeded my expectations because of "my people." The discipline with which I have prepared myself to start back to school for my master's was challenged by "my people." Even though I have confidently walked into all of these things on my own, my community has come in with guns blazing, ready to watch me succeed and challenge me deeper than I have felt capable. I owe so much of my perseverance to them, and I want you to experience that as well.

To have someone in your corner, cheering you on, pushing you further than you want to go, and inspiring you by their own life, that is one of the biggest blessings to have on this side of heaven.

If I haven't been convincing enough, I want to give a couple of stories that show the type of friends you should have on your team and the type of friend you should be. It was around September of 2019, and "desolate" is the best word to describe my state of mind. I felt totally abandoned, hopeless, and like no life was growing in my soul, or at least not like it used to. I was taking an art class at the time, and I asked a friend to come meet me after class. I had kept everything bottled up for months, and I really just wanted to throw up every word I could think of to someone to let them know how I was feeling; I remember being not able to take it anymore and just wanting an escape, advice, something, anything from someone other than my own mind. So I reached out to my friend Ben. For the record, Ben was a metal arts friend of mine and one of the most talented artists I knew. We had walked through four years of college together and shared many deep talks around religion, theology, love, politics, and likely anything else you can think of. He knew me well, and he knew my art even better.

As artists, we choose to let our work speak for itself because I think most of us are afraid to say the words. I always say, "Art is what words don't have the depth to say." So for him to know my art, to know my artist's statement, and for him to have walked through four years of art school with me, I knew I could say less, and he would still understand where I was coming from.

We met late on a Tuesday night. I remember it like it was yesterday. I had clay all over me from head to toe. I was wearing jeans, an old T-shirt, and work boots. He was wearing virtually the same but covered in metal dust and weld splatters. He looked at me and said, "So, you wanna talk?" I reluctantly sighed and laughed simultaneously. We walked out of the studio and sat across from one another on a big couch in the art building. I began telling him what had happened, explaining how much deeper this wound was than I initially thought. "I'm a strong person," I said. "I knew I would be hurt if this ever happened, but not this hurt. I feel like I've totally lost who I am." The entire time as I spoke, he just listened, and his eyes looked like they were cutting through me. Halfway through I wished I would have continued to bottle all of this up because I felt more vulnerable and exposed with every word I let out. At the end of the conversation, I stopped talking, finally, and just looked at him and said, "What is wrong with me? I've never been in this dark of a place in my entire life. I feel completely consumed with thoughts that aren't mine, and I don't know how to escape."

I knew Ben had been through a very similar situation a couple of years back, and I watched him walk through that season of life. I knew, from a distance, how tough it was on him. So I asked him, "How did you get through it?"

Ben looked at me and said, "I woke up every morning, and I screamed. I didn't look at myself but once in months. The time I did look, the life was completely sucked out of me. My blue eyes were as dull as ever, no light in them. Empty. People would ask me how I was doing, and I would just say, 'I'm doing!' I was okay with not being okay."

I dropped my head and for a second felt a sigh of relief that he was willing to open up to me, something he rarely did with anyone, just like I had done with him. It was almost as if I immediately felt our friendship deepen into something more intimate right before my eyes.

Then before I could say another word, he looked back at me, in the eyes this time, and said, "Katlyn, the sooner you let the old version of yourself go, the sooner you will begin to let go of the past too. You aren't the same anymore, and you won't ever be that Katlyn again." I remember feeling tears well up in my eyes, and I tried with everything I had to pull them back in.

He was right. Looking back now, I am so far from the person I was then, but even at that moment, I had already begun the pivotal changes that would spring me forward onto the path I am on now. He could listen to me talk, watch my body language, hear my questions, hear how my heart had changed, hear how I talked about God had changed, and know that I was different, and he knew the following year would bring even more changes to who I was. I didn't know that, but for some reason I believed him. This was about letting an old Katlyn go. A Katlyn that I had outgrown. Another person didn't solely cause the deep wounding

I felt. My subconscious knew it was time for the next journey, the next chapter. It was beckoning me onward, and I was still holding on to the Katlyn I loved so dearly. I loved her life, her innocence, her thoughts, her naivety, her dreams and goals, her plans. I loved everything about her.

But she wasn't risking anything like I am now.

She wasn't running full force into the next dream because all she could see was the one that had failed right in front of her eyes.

To this day, I cannot thank Ben enough. I don't think he understands how much that conversation impacted me, and unless he reads this book, maybe he never will.

At that moment, he showed me the rawness of friendship, the vulnerability, the transparency, the odd encouragement, and the tough love of what was coming next for me if I so allowed it. I don't think I would have chosen self-discovery and the path to "a new me" that I chose if it wasn't for him and others like him guiding me along the way when I only had maybe 10 percent to give. Thank God they were there to give the other 90 percent.

This last story I want to tell is from the opposite perspective. Fast forward about a year from my conversation with Ben, I have a very close friend who had recently gone through an emotional catastrophe, if you will, in a relationship. The relationship ended, but he was hanging on for dear life. This friend—I'll leave him nameless—knew that I had a relationship with the woman that had recently ended things with him. One night he sent me a voice note begging me to talk to her for him. This conversation had happened many times before, but I think this was the moment that sent me overboard. In the voice note, he said, "Will you please just fight for me and tell her how much I love her?"

I remember sitting there and hearing the pain, hurt, and tone of almost begging in his voice. I thought for a moment about saying yes and just doing what he had asked. I mean, wouldn't a friend do something like this? And at that moment, I realized that I would be taking the easy way out and that I wouldn't be truly fighting for him as he asked. I thought it through long and hard and sent a voice message back saying absolutely not.

I can't recall the voice note word for word, but I remember telling him that by being a true friend I couldn't let myself beg for someone else to love him. The best way for me to fight for him wasn't to beg her to come back; it was to stand up to him and tell him that he is worthy of someone he doesn't have to chase. He is worthy of reciprocated love and respect. Even though his self-esteem was at an all-time low, I wasn't going to allow him to belittle the person he was. I wasn't going to allow him to beg for scraps of love from others. I remember thinking how harsh the voice note I sent back to him was but how relieved I felt to have sent it. I ended it by telling him that I loved him and how I was only saying all of these things out of tough love because I would have wanted someone to do the same for me.

It's not that he has no confidence; it's that he was in a season of life and had just come out of a circumstance that had consumed him and hidden the self-esteem he once had. He was recovering and vulnerable, and, as a friend, I could not allow him to lessen his worth because of one person. He may not have fully understood or agreed then, but I know one day in the future, he will realize how hard it was for me to truly fight for him in the way he deserved.

Later on, I received a "Thank you for fighting for me," and that was all the satisfaction I needed to know I did the right thing. I expected an angry response, but I got a humble, "Thank you." Sometimes in life, we are too blinded to make the choices we should, and those moments are when we have to rely upon the friends we have chosen to help guide us in the right direction. I can't stress enough the importance of having a group of friends willing to give you tough love and being a friend willing to give tough love.

Take the time to invest in this area of your life, and I promise you, you will see growth in yourself and joy arise like you wouldn't believe. Ask yourself who are the five people you spend the most time with. Are you happy with being the average of those people? If not, now is the time to change it.

"YOUR JOY IS YOUR SORROW UNMASKED. AND THE SELFSAME WELL FROM WHICH YOUR LAUGHTER RISES WAS OFTENTIMES FILLED WITH YOUR TEARS."

– KAHLIL GIBRAN

ENDURANCE

Endurance: the fact or power of enduring an unpleasant or difficult process or situation without giving way.

This word has been the deepest expression of my life throughout this season I am currently in. For the past few months, I have constantly been reminded to "endure" in the moments when I feel the weakest.

Isn't it funny how the word "endurance" has a nice feeling attached to it, kind of a strong and confident spirit about it; however, to "endure" seems way more daunting, painful, and scary? I think there is a reason for that. People love to be proud of the act of doing something or even the thought of it, but when it comes down to actually doing the challenging task at hand, many of us bail out. When "-ance" is added to the end of the word, the meaning changes from being a verb, actually enduring, to a noun, meaning "a state of" enduring. "I am enduring this pain" sounds a lot different than "I am handling this pain with endurance."

To get to the point, we have to begin to take the verbs we most closely identify with every day and start morphing those into ways that we can describe ourselves. Enduring hardship leads to a continual spirit of endurance throughout the many other areas of our lives. When it comes to growth, there is no way around it that endurance and perseverance are the two levers that must be pulled at some point in the process, and typically they are the last ones we ever reach for. We always hear stories about people who have gone through intense hardship, adversity, and pain but who came out with a completely new outlook on life and learned much about themselves throughout the process. We always hear those stories about being victorious after the hardship is over, how the person endured with strength and came out on top in the end. We are always quick to dial in, quick to give a round of applause at the end and a "Wow, what an inspiration," but we are never quick to jump into those times ourselves even if we knew that those times could quite possibly spring our lives forward in remarkable ways. Even if we knew that some of the most painful experiences of our lives would lead us to the most beautiful destinations, we would still be reluctant to jump in with excitement about where the journey will take us.

I want to encourage you, whether you are currently in a season of pain and disappointment or your life is going great at the moment. You want to be fully equipped when the harsh storms of life hit; having a spirit of endurance will liberate you and carry you through till the end.

IT'S SUNNY HERE

This is for those of you who are coasting through life nicely at the moment. I want to challenge you to stop for a moment, take a deep breath, and be thankful. Your life probably isn't perfect, nor does it come free from troubles and daily struggles, but be thankful that it is where it is. Often in life, we choose to see the bad, choose to see the tiny things that are so wrong, and we never take time to truly be grateful. That goes for all of us. Even in the midst of suffering, it could always be worse. One of my best friends says, "You find what you are looking for."

So if you are looking for the bad, you are going to find it. If you are looking for the good, you are going to find it. Choose to notice and be thankful for the good. Although life may be at ease for you right now, the storms of life are inevitable, and I am sure you have already been through a few and know that one will be on its way sooner rather than later. However, this time I want you to be fully equipped to handle what comes your way. This is your time to prepare for battle and collect your arsenal, so when the storms hit, when the war rages on, you are prepared to stand strong.

Oftentimes in life we fail to prepare for things, and when they hit us, we are overwhelmed and completely consumed by them. At this point, take inventory of where you stand in terms of doubts, fears, and insecurities that could lead to a storm in your life. Address those issues and continue to become self-aware to help prevent what could have been a disaster. Take time to journal about where you are in life, how God is providing, and how great things are going. Write down these moments so that when the storm hits, you can look back and remember how faithful God was to you then and have faith that He will provide like this for you again. We worship a caring God who is faithful beyond belief. He has blessed you in the past, and He will bless you in the future, but don't forget to thank Him in the present.

THE CLOUDS ARE CLEARING

Now, for those of you who have just recently come out of a storm: You made it. It doesn't matter if it was a win where you crossed the finish line victoriously, not too much sweat and with a first-place medal now hung around your neck or whether it was you finishing dead last, crawling to the finish line, and everyone else has already gone home. Either way, you finished. And I guarantee you can look back and see the things you learned and ways you grew from this time of hardship. And if not, you're not looking hard enough.

Just as I encouraged those who aren't facing a storm at the moment to write down their many blessings and things they are grateful for to look back on in the future, I want to encourage you to write down the things you have learned after weathering this storm. There are many articles and studies out there that reference the importance of writing things down. Our memories tend to get so foggy, and even if the memory stays, sometimes it is hard to bring back all of the details, the full emotion, and the best recollection of what really happened.

So write down what you just went through.

Write down what felt like agony and what you did to combat it.

Write down what you learned about yourself, how you handle conflict, and how you go into self-preservation mode when you feel attacked.

Analyze these details about yourself that you would never have known without going through a storm like this.

How did you find your way back?

Who was there for you when you felt so alone?

What did you do to feel those tiny moments of pleasure again, even if they were only there for a second?

Write down even the things you would never want to tell anyone else.

Write down those moments when you felt like you couldn't do it anymore and what gave you the endurance to keep pushing.

Those are the things that are invaluable to your life. Those are the reasons you believe life is worth living, and you would have never truly known the value of them without going through this storm life sent your way. And even if it all seems like a blur to you, the most important thing you learned through enduring all of this is now you truly understand how to appreciate things when they are going well. You learned not to sweat the small stuff and to choose your battles wisely because some are just not worth fighting. You learned to choose your words wisely because the things people say can't be taken back. You learned how great that friend is or how great those friends and family members were that helped you get back on your feet every time you collapsed back down to the floor. Or maybe you learned that your friends aren't who you thought they were and you need to invest in some new ones.

We can never truly appreciate the good until we experience the bad. We can never know true joy until we have experienced deep sorrow. And the things in life that bring us the most joy are also the things that can lead us to the most pain, so we have to learn to appreciate them while we can and mourn them when they're gone. A piece from Kahlil Gibran's *The Prophet* expresses this concept beautifully:

Then a woman said, Speak to us of Joy and Sorrow.
And he answered: Your joy is your sorrow unmasked.
And the selfsame well from which your laughter rises
was oftentimes filled with your tears. And how else can
it be? The deeper that sorrow carves into your being,
the more joy you can contain. Is not the cup that holds
your wine the very cup that was burned in the potter's
oven? And is not the lute that soothes your spirit the
very wood that was hollowed with knives? When you
are joyous, look deep into your heart and you shall
find it is only that which has given you sorrow that is
giving you joy. When you are sorrowful, look again
in your heart and you shall see that in truth you are
weeping for that which has been your delight. Some of
you say, "Joy is greater than sorrow," and others say,
"Nay, sorrow is the greater." But I say unto you, they
are inseparable. Together they come, and when one sits
alone with you at your board, remember that the other
is asleep upon your bed. Verily you are suspended like
scales between your sorrow and joy. Only when you
are empty are you at standstill and balanced. When the
treasure-keeper lifts you to weigh his gold and silver,
needs must your joy or your sorrow rise or fall.

Remember this and encourage someone else who has had
their joy replaced with sorrow. Believe in them and help guide

them to the finish line because by having been there before, your compassion and empathy far outweigh anyone else's who can't relate. Take your victory and go cheer on someone else who is struggling to make it there. Your understanding and encouragement might be just what they need to take the next step forward.

THE RAIN KEEPS COMING

For those of you currently in a storm, I am right there with you. I chose to write this chapter when I was fighting through the dark thoughts of my own mind, the doubts and fears that so often come back to leave me feeling desolate, abandoned, and so very tired. I wanted to write this chapter when I myself had to choose endurance over running from my problems, perseverance over giving up, and strength when all I feel is weakness.

Before going any further on this topic, I want you to know that you are valuable.

Your life is worthy of being lived. Not just survived but LIVED. Sometimes it's the small things in life that knock us down, and it seems like they just keep coming. Other times it is a massive hurricane you never expected that completely wipes you out. Either way, the days when we feel like we can't take any more, when life isn't worth living, these are the times when we need to dig down the deepest and find the power of endurance.

No one has ever finished a race and regretted making it to the finish line. No one has ever sat in the line at Krispy Kreme for an hour but regretted it once they finally got to taste that freshly made donut (the Hot Light was on, of course). No one gets up out of bed in the morning, chooses to make their day meaningful and productive, but regrets it when they lie down to go to bed that night. Endurance might mean fighting off the lies from the enemy, thoughts of fears and insecurity, and facing a life you aren't enthused to live at the moment. I promise you it will be worth it. I promise myself right now that it will be worth it.

We are too quick to give up, too quick to lie down, and too quick to let the enemy win. Whatever that thing is that is stealing your joy today, don't let it win. You are too beautiful, too intelligent, too hard-working, too loved, and too special to let someone or something steal your joy. Happiness comes and goes, but inner joy for life is something we have to choose to stay.

As we discussed in the first chapters, feelings do not dictate the truth.

The truth is the truth no matter how we feel about it. And the truth is that you are making a difference in the world, so don't stop now because of this.

The truth is that a season is only a season, and this too shall pass.

The truth is that one day you will look back and be so proud of yourself for enduring one of the most challenging times in your life.

The truth is that one day, this thing that is hurting you and causing you so much pain will be the very thing that helps you grow into the incredible person you desire to become.

This very thing that gives you deep sorrow will one day be something that causes rejoicing in your life. A season is just a season, and if we truly want to grow, we have to say, "Bring on the rain."

I HAVE LEARNED THAT
TO GET WHAT WE
WANT, USUALLY THE
EXACT OPPOSITE IS
WHAT WE NEED.

SERVANTHOOD

I don't know about you, but when life gets hard, the last thing I want to do is serve other people. We talked about transparency earlier in this book, and the honest, transparent truth is that I am the type who always wants to fix her own problems and issues before she helps anyone else with theirs. I used to think to myself, "I am not in a state that is properly prepared to help anyone else." I remember thinking how the act of me not helping anyone when I was a mess myself was a good gesture. I was doing others a favor by not interfering in their lives because I was not credible or adequate, especially in that specific moment. This is one of those things that I truly convinced myself of. Until I realized the actual truth, this is a prime example of something that didn't change until my perception changed. Until then, my definition of what was good didn't change.

Back to the Maurice Nicoll quote: "Truth must enter and grow in a man before he can change the direction of his will—that is before his feeling of what is good can change." This all goes back to self-awareness and allowing yourself to realize that the so-thought "truth" of yesterday might not be the truth of today, and what I have believed this entire time was never actually true to start with.

Because, in reality, the value of my servanthood should never be measured by my adequacy in helping. It should be measured by my willingness to serve.

And to be honest, even when life is going great, I am typically "too busy" to make an intentional effort to reach out to others. I might volunteer here and there if I have some free time or give a friend a ride somewhere if they need it, but rarely do I intentionally make an effort to serve others, whether in big ways or small ways. Servanthood needs to be a part of our character, something that we have nurtured into our way of being, not something we simply partake in a few times a year to feel good about ourselves or to post for likes on social media. Some people are naturally better and desire to serve more than others. Regardless, we all have to make an *intentional* effort to serve because the selfishness in each of us demands our time more than anything else. And the key word here is "intentionally."

Later on, we will dive into a deeper understanding of intentionality and how it can completely reshape our way of living, but until then, servanthood is a great example of a way we can begin to intentionally pursue things that will benefit our headspace.

There are many reasons why we shy away from serving others, but I believe the biggest one is that we subconsciously question why we would help someone else, invest our time in others, when we have so much on our own plate to take care of. We have so much going on in our own lives, and we think when we do get a second to stop and breathe, we owe ourselves personal time to relax and do what we want. We *deserve* our "me time." We *deserve* to spend the weekends doing what we want because we spent an entire five days putting in work for something or someone else. Now I'm not saying personal time is never needed or spending time doing what you love is a bad thing. Doing what you love is a great thing!

But the issue is, we constantly create a habit of choosing ourselves instead of choosing others, and that is when we start to fall off track without ever noticing.

Going back to entitlement, we all have this selfish nature inside us that tells us to choose ourselves whenever possible. It tells us that we deserve to have our needs and wants met. It tells us that if someone or something is not benefiting us in any way we should move on and find something or someone that will. It tells us to only go the extra mile for those who will go the extra mile for us. Just think about it. You read poems and quotes and music lyrics all about choosing yourself. We grow up hearing, "Do what makes *you* happy," and we are instilled with the idea that happiness can only come from things we create for ourselves. Happiness only comes from our hobbies, our friends, our dreams, and our passions.

We have such a shallow idea of happiness, and we are too scared to ever explore anything otherwise. I have learned that to get what we want, usually the exact opposite is what we need. I have learned that when all I can think about is myself, my struggles, and the issues that are overwhelming me at the moment, the best thing I can do is listen to someone else and help them with their circumstances.

I have learned that leaving myself and all of my thoughts behind and intentionally choosing to help someone else with theirs gives me the break, the rejuvenation, and the purpose I need to give me the confidence to overcome my battles when I am ready to revisit them. So often when I choose to help others instead of myself, the rewards are far greater than I could have ever imagined.

We have to decide to go against the grain, against societal norms, to experience the freedom that not many get to experience. A life pursuing growth is never easy, and there will be countless sacrifices you have to make along the way, but once you realize how much better life is, all the sacrifices will have been worth it. To you now, giving up your time, putting your emotional burdens to the side, and intentionally choosing someone else over yourself might seem daunting and not worth your while, but when you get to the other side of this and look back on your past self, you will see how greatly you benefited and how the character you have now developed is a version of you that you will be forever grateful for.

Whether we consciously realize it or not, time is the most valuable thing we can give someone. We can easily give money to others. We can easily donate our old clothes to a shelter. What's hard is taking the time to invest in helping others when we know there is nothing we will get back in return. What we don't realize is how beneficial servanthood is to us and how the act of serving is sometimes what we deeply need the most for ourselves.

There is something so powerful and uplifting about choosing someone else over yourself.

In November of 2019 I was asked by a "social media friend", as we had only met in person a handful of times, to go with him and another close friend of his to Cambodia. The trip was to help a family that he had met through missionary work build their own ministry in their local village. That's all he told me, so I basically had no clue what I was getting myself into other than helping people in Asia with their ministry efforts. This friend knew I loved to travel, but also knew that this was a shot in the dark as any sane person would not go on a trip halfway around the world with someone they barely knew. Not only that, but the trip was only six weeks away. Lucky for him, I was not a sane person in those days, and any way to escape my current life and runaway for a while, I was going to take it. So I did. I remember the three of us meeting in the Detroit airport for the final two legs of our flights. I flew in from Kentucky, Chase flew in from Texas, and my soon-to-be new friend Christian flew in from Florida. We got on the plane and were off to South Korea first, then to Cambodia. This was also my first time in Asia, so every aspect of this trip was foreign to me. From traveling and getting to know my new friends, one of which became a best friend to me, and spending nearly two weeks helping another person pursue their dreams, I was the happiest I had been in a long time. Vuthy and Connie took me in and treated me as if I was part of their family from the day we arrived in Cambodia. Barely anyone in the village spoke English, but no language barrier can come between acts of love and acts of service. We ate every meal together. We laughed uncontrollably together. We worked all day together. And we focused on everyone but ourselves those two weeks. We slept in beds with rats running through the mattresses, we showered with buckets of cold water (with plenty of frogs jumping in the buckets), we fought off spiders bigger than our hands (I'm not exaggerating), we ate the bare minimum (usually mystery meat soup with rice), and we loved every second of it. Because nothing makes you feel as alive and purposeful as seeing your acts of servanthood help someone else achieve their dreams. Nothing brings you to your knees and makes you experience humility more than when you see someone else with far less than you, who is willing to give more than you ever have. Nothing makes you more grateful for your life, and all its shortcomings, than to hear stories from someone who had walked through the depths of suffering and who had come out saying "God provide" like my dear friend Vuthy had. It reminds me of a quote I came across recently in *Has Christianity Failed You?* by Ravi Zacharias that reads, "A friend of mine in India, who lives in a meager little place, once told me he always prays for America because "it must be so hard to trust in God when you already have so much."" This could not have been truer regarding my experience in Cambodia. I know that the people I met in Cambodia gave me far more than I gave them. I went there to serve them, but by doing so, they served me. They changed my perspective. They showed me what true love looks like. They showed me that love can break every single barrier and that sometimes, and I would argue most times, having less really means having more.

That trip taught me that sometimes we are so constantly wrapped up in our own problems that we don't realize how small they actually are. Pain is pain, and everyone experiences it differently, but sometimes it takes us helping others, listening to others, to realize how blessed we are. So many times in life we get caught up, only seeing in our small scope. If we zoom out, we realize that our issues are so small compared to what we should be worried about or what we should be focused on helping others with.

Take a moment to think about the most joyful people you know.

Are they the ones who would go to the ends of the earth for you or for anyone?

Are they the type to be there for you at all hours of the night?

Are they the type to continuously give sacrificial love to others even when they don't deserve it?

You likely answered yes to all of these questions because people with a servant's heart reap benefits that are unmet by any amount of happiness received from selfishness. The irony in all of this is that by choosing to live a life of servanthood, the humility, wisdom, pure joy, and confidence you receive are worth so much more than what you thought you were giving up. By giving up your time for someone or something other than yourself, something so valuable, you receive back tenfold the reward.

Giving truly is receiving.

The last thing that ties in with servanthood is sacrifice. Ultimately, when we choose to serve others, we are sacrificing something from ourselves. We are choosing to give up our desires and replace them with someone else's, and to most of us, that doesn't sound too appealing. The way to true happiness for ourselves is through others' happiness, but we as humans struggle to grasp that concept of sacrificial love—whether it is with a friend or, even more importantly, a spouse, fiancé, boyfriend, or girlfriend.

I think sometimes we get confused about what it means to sacrifice for others when we don't understand and when things don't make sense.

In the next chapter, I'll talk even more about how to respond when life doesn't make sense, but for now, let's use the perfect example of sacrificial love. I think we see the picture of Jesus on the cross and forget that the King of all kings became a servant for us. He was a living sacrifice for us. I think we forget to apply this kind of quality Jesus saw in our lives and are constantly searching to fulfill our own desires, reach our own highest level of individuality, that we forget what true love is all about.

Sacrifice.

True love sees someone for their insecurities, fears, past, and doubts and decides they will joyously pick up that baggage and carry it with them. When we look at Jesus, we see the perfect picture of someone who saw our burdens, scars, pain, and even though He didn't deserve because He was absolutely perfect, He went to the cross anyway.

There will be times in our lives when sacrificing a particular thing seems like too much. There will be times when we just don't understand people. We don't understand their fears, insecurities, or why something upsets them. We aren't going to be able to recall their past and those moments that have made them who they are. We all react to things differently. We all have a different perspective. But if you love someone, you choose them anyway. You choose to compromise or sacrifice for them. Because true love is never about you. True love is about the other person. And if we all have that attitude towards one another, we will begin to see the most genuine expression of love there possibly is. We will all be selflessly choosing someone else just as they are selflessly choosing us.

So make the choice now to express sacrificial love to the person or people you care about. Make the choice now to become more intentional about putting servanthood at the top of your priority list. Stop letting the selfish thoughts we have every day overtake you because even though it sounds like getting what you want, you could be getting much better by putting someone else above yourself.

As I said before, I have learned that sometimes to get what we want, the exact opposite is what we need. And even though your focus might be on yourself, know that the benefits of serving someone else will far outweigh the time you spend on fixing yourself.

Selfishness is a mighty warrior always fighting for your heart, don't let it win.

THAT DESIRE IN YOUR HEART QUESTIONING THE MEANING OF LIFE, ABOUT YOUR PURPOSE HERE, ISN'T GOING TO SATISFY ITSELF WITHOUT AN INTENTIONAL PURSUIT TO FIND THE TRUTH.

FAITH

I would be amiss if I wrote this entire book and didn't include a chapter on faith.

The thing I have pursued the hardest, wrestled with the most, and have seen the most growth in throughout the last two years has been my faith.

Going back to something I mentioned in Chapter One, I want to reiterate the importance of the process not the end result. I feel as though we grow up striving to find the truth regarding an afterlife, purpose, creation, and every other aspect that gives meaning to this life. We are pressured to choose something based on fear-tactics, family ritual, or the culture we are surrounded by. The goal is never the process but solely focuses on the end result. Once you found what you believe to be true regarding your spirituality, the journey stops and you feel at ease knowing you're right and everyone else with an opposing view is wrong.

The point of this chapter isn't for me to force my beliefs upon you, but rather to urge you to not stop once you've solidified your answer- to be open to learning more, asking questions, and not being afraid of the answers you find. If there is one answer about those things I mentioned, an afterlife, purpose, creation, etc, shouldn't we all be striving to learn more about it? To get closer and closer to the truth? That desire in your heart questioning the meaning of life, about your purpose here, isn't going to satisfy itself without an intentional pursuit to find the truth.

Regarding faith, I have a message for two groups of people.

For those of you who are still wrestling with your religious/ spiritual beliefs or want nothing to do with any of them, choose to take the hard road and continue searching. Once again, "All find what they truly seek." If you earnestly search for the answers, you'll find them. Maybe you aren't concerned with the answers you'll find, but even so, the journey itself will prove to be worth the effort. From the beginning of humanity people have had a longing to know the truth about how and why we were created. This unifying desire in our hearts has to mean something. C.S. Lewis says, "If we find ourselves with a desire that nothing in this world can satisfy, the most probable explanation is that we were made for another world." For me, the search unleashed things, and still is releasing things, in me that I never knew existed. My mind has expanded. My logic and reasoning skills have improved. I ask better questions. I find holes in other people's arguments as well as my previous stance on topics. I listen to others who have questions, because I've likely had the same ones. I have grace for others, knowing we're all doing the best we can with the information we have. My confidence in what I do believe has grown into something that is solid ground, able to be the foundation for everything else in my life.

I would urge you, whether it's complacency, carelessness, or fear of what you may find, don't stop reading, studying, listening, meditating, and reaching out into the vastness of the metaphysical to ask for answers to your questions. There's not a doubt in my mind that you will receive an inkling of something that will invigorate you to keep going. The journey itself is worth it, regardless of where you'll end up (even though I have my guesses of where the road will take you).

For my fellow Christians, I want you to know that by settling into our beliefs because of how we were raised or even coming to grips with it on our own in later years, we are doing ourselves a huge disservice by not continuing to learn more about God. By learning more about Him, we are inevitably learning more about ourselves as we were created in His image. Not only that, the constant reshaping of your idea of God will reaffirm your faith and draw you nearer to Him, nearer than most people are willing to go. C.S. Lewis (I quote him a lot, I know) says, "My idea of God is not a divine idea. It has to be shattered time after time. He shatters it Himself." There is always more to learn about God.

I've realized that my problem was that I was content with the idea of God the church gave me or maybe the one I desired to have myself- the one that sounded nice once I conjured it up myself. When life came and knocked me off my feet the questions I had bubbled to the surface and wreaked havoc on the faith I thought I had bolted down. Without a continual pursuance to know His character better, *truly* know Him, for the parts I may not understand as well as the ones I do, I will be shattered time and time again when His character surprises me.

I wrote a journal entry a year or so ago that addressed God and said that I wanted to know every detail about Him. As much as my minuscule brain could comprehend. I wanted to know the real Him, not simply the God that Christians write songs about. I wanted to know more about the severe mercy He shows us by doing hurtful things only He can understand. I wanted to better understand where my opinion stood on inclusivism, exclusivism, and annihilationism, and even if I may never know which is the correct answer I wanted to be able to give reasoning as to why I believe what I do. I said that I wanted to know why it felt like sometimes He wasn't around but others I couldn't escape His presence. I wanted to know if things were a coincidence or if they truly were divine intervention in my life. I wanted to know how much of my life was dictated by me, others around me, or His plan for me.

I had many questions that I had buried deep inside me from such a young age that were bursting to come out. You can ask my mom about this. I remember running to her, in tears, asking her why Satan didn't get a second chance to go to Heaven but I did. Why Judas went to Hell because without him betraying Jesus we wouldn't have had a savior. I was an inquisitive little girl, to say the least, who never took anything she saw as truth without proper evidence- who questioned everything. I still have those tendencies and sometimes they benefit me greatly, but other times they cost me peace of mind and restful nights. It may be in my nature to always want to know the truth, but I've learned that God doesn't shiver at the sound of my questions. God doesn't make excuses or try and hide the answers from me. There are some things our human brains may never be able to grasp, but God has steered me in the direction that has given me either answers, clarity, or peace about the subject at hand. And along the way, I feel as though He's applauded my effort to know Him better.

Not too long ago I was really struggling with what I believed about God. I had stopped going to groups I attended frequently, I stepped away from church, and I completely stopped spending time in scripture. With that being said, I still spoke with God on the daily, but it was more of arguing my thoughts than it was praising Him or thanking Him for anything. I don't recommend having my attitude towards Him, but I do recommend being real with Him. Whatever that looks like where you're at.

I had a friend who knew I was studying, researching, asking, begging, and yelling for answers and she totally changed my perspective one day when she said, "Katlyn, how remarkable is it that you're fighting so hard for your relationship with the Lord. You're truly working things out with Him and it's so admirable. Not many people go this deep into their faith." I was so confused as the entire time I had felt a heap of shame and guilt on my shoulders for my questions, for my bitterness towards God, and for my negative attitude towards everything I once believed. But she was right. I wasn't giving up, and I wasn't running from my questions anymore. I wasn't afraid of finding out that my faith was a lie if that's the conclusion I came to. I wasn't afraid of being judged by the church for not showing up. I wasn't afraid of telling people that I was wrong if that's what I discovered. I wasn't scared of converting to another religion or no religion at all. All I cared about was finding the truth.

If you haven't noticed the trend yet, that search for truth regarding my spirituality, my relationship with God, also bled into the search of finding my true self. When we search for the truth, we always find it. When we learn the proper skills, challenge our own beliefs, and let the fear of being wrong go, the truth shines bright right before our eyes.

By learning more about the author of this world, I learned more about the author of my life. I learned that I have a purpose, a reason to be taking up space here. I learned that the things I do and say make a difference here and have the potential to affect the lives of anyone and everyone I come in contact with. I learned that I have a duty to engage in self-discovery because my destiny relies upon it. And I learned that I must continue searching for the Truth if I ever wanted to have a real picture of who Katlyn was supposed to be, who she can still be.

If your faith has been messy, don't give up on it. If you have questions, don't stop seeking the answers. If life doesn't make sense, maybe it's not God, maybe it's your perception that's making things hard to see.

I want to end this chapter with a story that I hope can encourage you if you find yourself questioning the motives of God.

There is a sweet lady, I'll call her Lisa, who works in the office building next to my mom. She and my mom have been friends for years now, and this lady is an incredible woman of faith who always tries to be obedient when she hears the call of God in her life. She came into my mom's office the other day and began to tell a story that she said she felt so embarrassed of, something she didn't want to share but felt like she should. She began to say that a man she knew was really struggling financially. He had four children, and the mother was not around.

Lisa said she felt God telling her to give this man money even though her real estate business was not on the upside at the moment, and she was even struggling financially herself. She said she truly felt this strong pull to write a check to this man for a generous amount of money, so she wrote out $3,000 on the check and handed it to the man.

A few weeks went by, and she heard that the man had booked a cruise for him and the four children to go on. She said she has never felt so much anger, she could not believe that he would use the money for this, and she also couldn't believe that she misjudged the voice of God to give someone like this money all while she herself was really struggling. She never said anything to the man but just felt so much anger and resentment towards him and questioned her discernment with God. A month passed, and the man and his children went on the trip.

Once they get back, it was not even a week that passed, and one of the young boys from the family was killed in a car accident. Lisa said she felt horrible and went to the funeral for the little boy, and while there she heard the father stand up and say how the only family vacation they had ever been on was the cruise and how the only photographs he had of him and his son were from that cruise.

Lisa said that she sat in the very back pew and wept the entire service. She said she had never felt so guilty for questioning God's guidance and that He always knows what He is doing. We can just never zoom out enough to see the big picture of His plans. Lisa said after that day, her real estate business picked up, and she sold more houses in the next couple of months than she had sold in the entire year, and every single one of them was a cash closing. My mom has also been doing real estate for a long time and has only had one cash closing in all her years of business.

There are some questions God may be graceful enough to give us answers to, but others I believe are too heavy for us to hold, so He must keep them for us. Focus this season, not on getting to the conclusion of where you believe truth lies, focus on the journey. Focus on the perseverance and humility it takes to always consider yourself a student- never able to learn enough about your purpose, your identity, and the One who created it all.

PART III

Intentionality

"IF YOU ARE NOT WILLING
TO RISK THE UNUSUAL,
YOU WILL HAVE TO SETTLE
FOR THE ORDINARY."

- JIM ROHN

CONSISTENCY DRIVES CREDIBILITY

I want to preface the title of this chapter by saying that what you read here might seem, at first, a little contradictory. "Consistency Drives Credibility" is the theme of this chapter, but I want to explain when consistency is important and when change or inconsistency is *more* important. There is a specific time and place for both, and in most situations, they are interconnected, flowing back and forth between one another. First of all, when I say "consistency," I don't mean simply staying consistent with the things you eat, your daily or weekly routines, or where you vacation every year. However, if you're only eating the same things and traveling to the same destinations every year, you miss out on so much the world has to offer, but that isn't the point. The point is that each of these, consistency and inconsistency, should both have their places in life, and we tend to get them completely mixed up—each dancing at their wrong turn.

Let's start with the beginning so I can describe when it's important not to be consistent. Life is constantly throwing us curve balls and expecting us to react. We are a very predictable species. As I've said before, I studied economics throughout college, and it was mind-blowing to me how truly predictable we are as consumers. A simple algorithm can predict our choices for an entire year. The worst part about this is that we can be swayed and misled into choices that are not even really of our own desires but are due to great marketing tactics and psychological manipulation. This is true in politics as well.

This is the first reason for us to choose not to be consistent with the day to day. This is when we need to truly take the time to evaluate our choices and decide, based on our values, the decision we want to make. We need to stop taking things for what they are, believing everything we see or hear, and actually begin to tear apart propaganda, tear apart arguments, and tear apart the things life has to offer us so that we can see each individual piece before claiming we want the thing itself, in its entirety.

Coming from the South, I grew up with many different traditions in my family. There were many things I did growing up because of the old-fashioned phrase, "That's how I was raised." Most of the traditions and values I gained from my family, friends, school, church, and culture were great; I've actually chosen to hold quite a few of them tightly, even now. However, there were many parts of my epistemology that I have spent time tearing apart now that I am older, and I did not come to any conclusions by taking those things as they were—whole. I came to the conclusion that I needed to let them go because I took the time to analyze and tear apart every detail of that habit, that mindset, that ideology, to see if any parts of it didn't make sense.

As my apologist friend Wes Mullins always reminds me, "We

have to start asking better questions."

We have to start breaking down our arguments to be able to see if they can hold up against anyone else's.

There are parts of my theology that have changed drastically in the last year. The ideas I had about God have changed, and things I have believed my entire life I had to let go so I could begin to grow closer to Him and even closer to myself. There are things I have believed about myself my entire life that I have recently had to let go of as well. Maybe they were true at one point, or maybe they never were—regardless, they are not true now. I am not that person now, and it's okay.

My opinions on things like politics, philosophy, culture, stereotypes, mental illness, morality have been either tweaked slightly or completely abolished and made new. I have met people my entire life, young and old, who have never done this kind of introspection.

Many times we get caught up in the day to day, the month to month, and the year to year. We let life pass us by without ever taking the time to evaluate ourselves, our decisions, our beliefs, our goals, and where all of those things are ultimately taking us. I talk with friends who once had their lives completely in order. They had big dreams; they were hard workers, but somehow their choices slowly started to alter their paths, and now they wake up to a life they never thought they would be living.

Although not all of our choices lead us to drastic changes in our lives, they shape not only who others think we are but also who we think we are ourselves. I had a conversation with my best friend and roommate the other day about this. She said, "Katlyn, do you think God created people that He knew would never reach their potential and chose to love them and create them anyways, or do you think everyone has the capability to reach their greatest potential in this life?"

We discussed this for a while, and my opinion is that every person has what it takes to live a life here on earth where they have maximized their overall well-being to the best that they could under their specific circumstances.

To not get off topic on a free will versus determinism argument, I will just say that we make small and large choices every day that can lead us closer or farther away from the true men and women we were created to be.

When I first began learning what self-awareness and intro-spection meant, I had this fiery urge not to stop until I uncovered all of my subconscious tendencies that needed to be evaluated or changed. I wanted to be the truest version of myself with every choice I made, every belief I held, to be backed up by some sort of truth I had intentionally found. I had this feeling that there was so much I was missing out on because I was blinded to the true me.

Choose to take inventory, to hear the ugly truth, the pretty truth, to understand the uncontrollables in your life, and become inconsistent in living a life that passes you by without any internal auditing done. Ask yourself what you believe and why you believe it.

Do the same with external elements. Those silly things I mentioned earlier, like the things you eat, the places you go for vacation or holiday, the books you read or movies you watch—those things, even though small and trivial, also have the ability to impact the richness we allow our lives to have. I was twenty years old before I ever flew in an airplane. I am now twenty-three years old, and this month I will have been to my fifteenth and sixteenth countries. Although we choose to invest our time and money in different areas, I have realized the joy and richness traveling has given me. I have learned and expanded my mind in many ways that twenty-year-old Katlyn never had the opportunity or the desire to, and for that alone, I am so grateful I chose to step out of my comfort zone and become inconsistent with my original ideas of what a "vacation" looked like. I wrote a post on my Instagram explaining this change I've had when it relates to traveling, and I think it fits perfectly with this chapter on when inconsistency finds its place.

Traveling is one of my very favorite things that this world has to offer. For me, it's a vice, a passion, a challenge, and a breath of fresh air. The feeling of experiencing a new place full of unseen territory, unmet people, and untapped adventure—the mystery of it all—sweeps me off my feet. Eating new foods, speaking new languages, learning about different cultures, and simply finding comfort in the uncomfortable is something I've always loved but never really let myself fully experience until this past year.

I was always hesitant to dive into a new place and experience it to the fullest. I was okay with staying in the safe bubble of no language barriers, of resorts or hotels, and of practicing the "American tourist" way of traveling.

As I just put down "To Shake the Sleeping Self" by Jedidiah Jenkins, I've come to realize how much I've evolved, and for the better, when it comes to traveling.

I want to encourage my travel pals to re-evaluate the way you experience a new place. Without expectations, without a sense of ethnocentrism, without the fear of messing up when trying the local language. Truly immerse yourself in the culture and lifestyle of where you are. Eat their food, learn their etiquette, bring only a backpack, and let them teach you how they live instead of coming to a new place simply to impose your own social norms just to make yourself feel more comfortable.

And for those of you too afraid to even travel to a place so foreign: DO IT.

Some of the most life-giving conversations I've ever had have been across borders in places so far from home.

Some of the times I've laughed the hardest have been with people who did not even speak my language.

Some of the most beautiful places my eyes have ever seen have been places I never thought I would go.

And some of the most pivotal revelations I've ever had have been many time zones away.

Moral of the story: "If you are not willing to risk the unusual, you will have to settle for the ordinary."
-Jim Rohn

[or another cheesy traveling quote]

Now onto the meat and title of this chapter—consistency drives credibility. As I have spent most of this book so far explaining the ways we should take inventory of our lives and make necessary changes in order to become the people we want to be, the people we were destined to be, now I want to highlight the importance of staying consistent with certain areas of our lives as well.

When I think about the people I look up to and admire the most, they all have one thing in common: consistency. The people I admire and strive to be more like are those that I know will always be there in a time of need, and not only that but will also continuously give me consistent advice that will guide me in the right direction. I would refer to these people as being extremely stable, constant, whole, confident, and strong. The irony behind this is that some of these people are the quietest and most soft-spoken friends and mentors I have. It seems that we have misconceived many words today in our English language, and I think "confident" and "strong" are two of those. Most of us think of an extroverted, sometimes judgmental, blunt personality that always has to put in their opinions during a conversation when we think of someone who is confident. Most of us think to be "strong," you need to be stoic in your actions and always cover up your emotions to preserve your appearance to others. Until you meet someone with true, genuine confidence, someone who has real strength, that is likely the image you will have in your head.

However, what makes someone strong and confident is their ability to be resolute in their epistemology, their beliefs, and the reason for their actions because they have intentionally set out to know themselves better than others could ever possibly know them. These people are the ones who know why they do what they do, and because of that, they have no doubts that they are leading others in an authentic direction as well. This doesn't mean we all don't need correction or redirection, but it does mean that because these people have chosen to be consistent in their actions, consistent in the way they speak of others, and consistent in how they handle their emotions, they have nothing to hide and nothing unpredictable to have to justify.

As I mentioned earlier, the people I cling to the most are the ones who truly are who they say they are. They are the ones who have shown me that time and time again. They are the people who have worked hard to better themselves and have no reason to feel insecure. I can't help but think of the people C.S. Lewis talks about in the last chapter of *Mere Christianity*.

Already the new men are dotted here and there all over the earth. Some, as I have admitted, are still hardly recognisable: but others can be recognised. Every now and then one meets them. Their very voices and faces are different from ours: stronger, quieter, happier, more radiant. They begin where most of us leave off. They are, I say, recognisable; but you must know what to look for. They will not be very like the idea of "religious people" which you have formed from your general reading. They do not draw attention to themselves. You tend to think that you are being kind to them when they are really being kind to you. They love you more than other men do, but they need you less. (We must get over wanting to be NEEDED: in some goodish people, especially women, that is the hardest of all temptations to resist.) They will usually seem to have a lot of time: you will wonder where it comes from. When you have recognised one of them, you will recognise the next one much more easily. And I strongly suspect (but how should I know?) that they recognise one another immediately and infallibly, across every barrier of colour, sex, class, age, and even of creeds. In that way, to become holy is rather like joining a secret society. To put it at the very lowest, it must be great fun.

This is the kind of person I strive to be every day, and equally as important, these are the kind of people I try to surround myself with every day. The older I get, the more I learn the irony of the way we live here on Earth. The humblest people of all would never call themselves humble. The richest people of all usually don't fit the world's definition of "rich" at all—sometimes even the opposite. And the strongest and most confident people might not look or seem strong or confident at all.

IF WE CARE ABOUT OUR
DREAMS, OUR GOALS, OR
LEAVING A LEGACY, WE HAVE
TO CARE ABOUT THE FUTURE
VERSION OF OURSELVES MORE
THAN WE CARE ABOUT THE
INSTANT GRATIFICATION WE
RECEIVE FROM THINGS HERE
AND NOW.

FOURTEEN YEARS WASTED

Just as consistent people seem to be deemed the most credible people, so are those who live their lives with undoubtable purpose. I have noticed over the last couple of years the qualities of people I gravitate towards the most, or at least admire the most, and those people are the ones who do what they say they are going to and know exactly why they are doing it.

As someone in her mid twenties, I have countless memories of people doing things "because [they] felt like it." That's the regular in college. You want to do something, so you do it. Your body enjoys it, you might have enough money in your bank account for it, someone else told you to, and once again, you just wanted to. I don't know if my brain is just wired differently, but I used to always be so intrigued by those people. How can they use "because I want to" as a justification for anything? Our hearts, minds, bodies, they are all so misleading to what we actually do need. How can they make those choices without even thinking twice or really narrowing down a better reason to do it?

Like I mentioned in the previous chapter, our actions are so easily predicted and usually predicted to do the thing we shouldn't or buy the things we shouldn't. My economics-major friends out there can skip ahead at this point, but in academia and among professional economists, you'll constantly hear the term "to maximize utility." It's a weird concept, but basically, economists quantify a person's level of overall well-being and try to figure out how a person's choices can maximize that. In simpler terms, take for example that person A's maximum utility is twenty (twenty being a number calculated by an economist, but just go with it for this example). The best way they can achieve that maximum level of overall well-being is by working X amount of hours per week, based on their earnings, and taking off Y amount of hours for leisure. Based on many other variables and scenarios, economists can then develop a lifestyle most suitable for any specific person. However, the majority of us never reach that maximum utility number of twenty (or whatever it is for you).

Many of us choose unhealthy options or work less (or more) than we should, thus lowering our utility. Of course, just like any other environment, fixed variables interfere with "the perfect formula" and can raise or lower the baselines simply based on the coefficient. Whether you are for extreme government intervention, a little government intervention, or none at all, you will hopefully still be able to see why and how some of our policies are implemented based on trying to improve society's overall well-being. For example, there are many articles you can find on the internet regarding hard and soft paternalism used around the world, some for good intention, some for bad. Paternalism is basically the government reaching over us to mandate rules and regulations in hopes to give us a better life; the issue with that is, against or in alignment with our will, it doesn't matter.

As someone who believes strongly in our freedoms, I am not here to argue that paternalism should or should not be taking place in our country, but before my fellow freedom fighters and libertarian friends get angry, I do see how some of it can be beneficial (emphasis on some).

A popular one to discuss is the cigarette tax in New York. If you're a smoker and have been to the Big Apple, I'm sure you have realized how inflated the cigarette price is there. This is a form of paternalism by mandating higher taxes in hopes that people will stop buying them and achieve overall better health. This not only helps the individual to raise their utility, but also to cheapen and lessen the risk in our insurance policies. It also relieves pressure in the healthcare industry, and the tax we receive off of them can then go for other government-funded projects to better improve our country.

My point isn't to get on an economic or political rant but to better inform you on how intentional some of these decisions are that are made by people whose jobs are to purposefully add value to our lives. If studying economics is not for you, maybe it can at least help reaffirm in you the importance of intentionality. Too many of us waste precious time by doing things that have no valid purpose. A better way to put it is, too many of us have our priorities misaligned and spend time on the activities that truly aren't going to get us where we want to go.

There is always a time and place for leisure, and many studies have even shown how Americans need more leisure for a happier, healthier life. However, *how* we experience leisure is important. I know people who relax by going on a run, reading a book, painting or doing something creative, fishing, hiking, baking, writing, and many more fruitful activities. These activities all work different muscles in our brain, give us release from tension, and improve other areas of who we are. But I know more people who indulge in excess social media, watching television, spending money that they don't have, eating too much of things they know they shouldn't, and plenty other activities that could be beneficial in moderation but not in excess. There are books on books showing the danger of our habits, how hard they are to break, and how important good ones are to achieve the goals we have set.

My point is that the things we do "just for fun" still should be adding some type of value to our lives. I would argue that most of them are, in the long run, hurting us more drastically than they are satisfying our instant gratification. In the next chapter I'll dig deeper into discipline and the importance of being not just okay but excelling in disciplining yourself. For now, I just want you to question your work time versus your leisure time.

Are you a workaholic?

Are you lazy and complacent?

Neither extreme is going to get you where your dreams want to take you. I laugh as I type this because no one would admit to being either, but if you're reading this book, you likely want some guidance. The least you can do is be honest with yourself.

According to my phone, the first reality check I had was that I was averaging around five hours a day looking at a screen. Do the math, and it's not too difficult to realize that I spend around

20 percent of my day looking at a screen. I also spend 34 percent of my day sleeping. So before I can accomplish anything, that is already over half of my day consumed. If you average five hours a day on your phone over the average lifespan of a person, I will likely spend around fourteen years looking at my phone by the time I die. Fourteen years of doing mostly meaningless scrolling on a device that brings me more comparison, sadness, anger, and weight to carry than any other outlet can.

Social media allows us to carry the burdens of many people's problems we were never meant to carry the weight of. Every heartbreak, every disaster, every scandal, every manipulated piece of information that slowly eats away at us is freely chosen to be seen by us. It sits on our fingertips almost every moment of the day. We are controlled by other people's opinions, desires, and narratives. Once again, the benefits of our phones, technology, and even social media are something to be thankful for. The fact that we can be in contact with our families or people from around the world is incredible. The fact that we can listen to music, read books, and find information quickly and seamlessly is such a blessing, but the ways we choose to use technology have taken over most of our lives and distorted them in ways they were never meant to be.

The worst part?

We don't only allow it; we welcome it.

We wake up and check our phones. We check our phones before bed, we sit scrolling on them during lunch, at dinner, on breaks throughout the day. We follow people on social media that we compare ourselves to. We "creep" on people we don't even like to see if their lives are better than ours or not. We post only what will make us look better and happier than everyone else in the world. We want all of the likes and all of the comments, and we watch who sees our Instagram stories. We get hurt or satisfied depending on the names we see. I can go on and on about the power we give the device in our hands. The device that is probably less than two feet away from you right now.

If you know me, you know I love sharing my travel stories, quotes, encouragement, and everyday moments on social media. But I have had to really challenge myself lately and have plenty of talks with myself around limitations, boundaries, and intentions when it comes to the life I share and the lives I scroll through on social media. My future self, my mental health, and simply my time is more important than that, and yours is too.

If you want to live a life in which your time is important, if you want to make a difference with the time you have here, follow these guidelines:

1. Start by asking yourself how you are maintaining work versus leisure.
2. Ask yourself how intentional you are about where you spend your free time.
3. Ask yourself if you spend your free time challenging yourself or growing some other area of your life or if your free time has a negative impact on your overall well-being, your personal utility.

4. How are the activities you are taking part in now going to benefit you in the long run?

If we care about our dreams, our goals, or leaving a legacy, we have to care about the future version of ourselves more than we care about the instant gratification we receive from things here and now. Put your phone down and love the people in front of you. Go for a run. Read a book. Write a book. Your future self will thank you for it.

WITHOUT DISCIPLINE, WE
ARE TAKING THE RISK OF
TESTING OURSELVES ONCE
WE ARE ACTUALLY ON THE
BATTLEFIELD, AND SADLY,
WE OFTEN CRUMBLE UNDER
PRESSURE.

DISCIPLINE

"Self-respect is the fruit of discipline; the sense of dignity
grows with the ability to say no to oneself."
- Abraham Joshua Heschel

B efore even finding this quote, I had a conversation with a
friend on this exact topic. He was telling me about his struggles with giving into cheap thrills and how easily tempted he is to
choose the easy way out in most situations. The conversation was
over text, and I responded "discipline" as quickly as my fingers
could type. The following text I sent said, "Extreme discipline.
& one can only be strong enough to discipline themselves if they
are confident in who they are. If not, they won't believe they can
do the hard things or resist the easy things. We have to constantly
build our confidence and build our discipline so that when times
come, we have all the weaponry to fight off those temptations.
Without true discipline, no one walks away from the cheap thrills."

Shortly after I sent that text, I started doing some research for
this chapter of the book and came across the quote from Abraham
Heschel, who explains what I was trying to say, but much more
eloquently. His quote even makes me question which comes

first—the confidence or the discipline. As I mentioned in the text to my friend, I believe that the only way to achieve true discipline is to see yourself as worthy enough to work hard for some things and refrain from others. I don't know many struggling addicts who value their life very highly or, in a deeper sense, even put much value on their inner self.

The confident people I know tend to be aware of where they stand on most things. They can give defend why they have to say no or justify why they say yes. They see themselves as valuable enough to do what is best for them at all times. However, in Heschel's quote, he says that starting with discipline will lead to confidence. Say yes to the experiences that you know will only better you, and say no to the experiences you know will only hurt you. Those choices will then *make* you a more confident individual. As he further explains, one's dignity is emboldened, and by the choices the person makes, they begin to see value and gratitude for themselves again. It seems that we are in a "which came first, the chicken or the egg" situation, but either way, discipline will either reap confidence or start from it.

I discuss all things confidence in the book's final pillar, but I think it's important to clarify here that just as confidence is something that is worked for, so is discipline. One of my closest friends throughout college struggled with an addiction to hard drugs before we met. He didn't just give them up quickly and easily. It was a hard-fought battle. He may have never relapsed as many people do, but for a long time, he fought the temptation, the indescribable urge, to use again. The further along he went in saying no to himself, the more his dignity and self-respect began to grow. For some of you, it may not be something as daunting. Or maybe it is. I don't know your personal story, but I know based on the nature of us humans, we tend to lean towards doing what feels good in the moment. Instant gratification is more readily available now than it ever has been. Not only do we choose to do what might be detrimental in the long run, we also tend to forgo the beneficial activities that would push us in the direction our inner consciousness wants us to go.

To be honest with you, I have never been a "bed maker." Throughout my childhood, into high school, and into college, I was never someone who woke up and made their bed. I always blamed it on being in art school because I don't know many creative people who enjoy making their bed; we tend to like organized chaos, or some of us, just chaos. I had heard all of the stories about how it builds good habits. I had read books that told me to make my bed. I even watched that long, famous speech by the military guy who starts by telling everyone to make their bed in the morning because it would be something they accomplished right at the beginning of their day. I loved all of that but simply wrote it off as just not being for me.

A few months ago something in me changed, and I don't think there has been more than a couple of days since then that I haven't made my bed. For me, it wasn't the thought of needing to feel like I accomplished something or that it looked nicer or that it would even build better habits. For me, I realized that I needed to work on discipline. I would make to-do lists and realize I would only

accomplish half of the things on the list, and some items would
be on there for months at a time. I noticed that I would wake up
and tell myself, "You need to go on a run today," and I simply
wouldn't go on the run. I thought to myself, "If I can't even obey
myself every day on trivial tasks, how do I expect myself to hear
out anyone else's advice or wisdom?" It worried me that I was
becoming one of those people who float through life with 10,000
tasks on a to-do list they never get done. Those people tend to
also be the ones who don't follow through with their big plans
and dreams for the future. If I can't tell myself what my body
needs and obey my orders, why would I listen to anything else I
or anyone has to say?

So I started making my bed. I don't even think about it anymore.
It is a discipline that shows me that I care and I am listening. I
don't have these hopes and dreams that are far off realities. My
"to-do's" are tangible and can be done. When I tell myself I am
going to do something now, I do it. I don't make empty promises
to myself, and hopefully, this bleeds out even into my social life.
I don't make empty promises to others either. Making my bed has
nothing to do with a routine or a schedule. It doesn't give me a
little confidence boost because I accomplished something. Rather,
it reminds me that I am a disciplined human being who knows how
to do something I don't necessarily want to do. It reminds me not
to give in to the easy things just because they are easy.

It's easy not to go on the run when I have no one else to hold
me accountable.

It's easy not to make my bed when no one sees my room or

sleeps in my bed but me.

It's easy to skip quiet time, eat unhealthily whenever I want, and sleep in on the weekends as late as I want when I have no one to report to.

We shouldn't only want to achieve or impress others by our discipline and hard work. We should want to impress ourselves. I don't want to only show up when others are around. I want to show up when it's just me.

Besides proving to yourself that you can do challenging things on your own, discipline also prepares you to avoid the cheap thrills this world has to offer. Food, for instance. If you have disciplined yourself to eat healthily and Saturdays are your only "cheat days," when someone asks you to go grab a pizza on a Thursday, you're a lot more inclined to say no than the person who is trying to live a healthier lifestyle but has yet to be strict with their diet. People tend to believe that the instant a person gives into something that isn't good for them, that's when they lose the battle. In reality, they lost the battle long before.

To get really personal for a second, the best example I have for this is regarding sex. I decided a long time ago, for multiple reasons, that I wanted to wait until I was married to have sex. I am almost twenty-four years old and have been in a couple of long-term relationships, so you can imagine it hasn't been the easiest thing to avoid. However, I have been able to keep that promise to myself because I have been disciplined for a long time and have known where I stand long before I am in a bedroom alone with a man. Thankfully, my previous relationships, during college and post-college, have respected that boundary, and some even felt the same as I did on the subject. It is something I have always made clear from the start, and at this point, I don't even dread the conversation.

My self-respect from being disciplined on this for years now has grown substantially, and I know that I am capable of keeping this promise. Ironically enough, the fact that I have been so confident on this subject has made it easy for the men I have spent time with to really appreciate and respect my decision. I've learned that when you own things about yourself, really own them confidently, not many people come attacking those things. Being disciplined allows you to know the battle is already won before you even get to the warzone. You have prepared yourself for this. You are equipped and skilled at this. Without discipline, we are taking the risk of testing ourselves once we are actually on the battlefield, and sadly, we often crumble under pressure.

To bring this chapter to a close, we can't forget that discipline doesn't come without intentionality. Unless you are willing to be intentional, to be purposeful about disciplining yourself, it will never come to fruition. Maybe making your bed isn't what will give you that understanding, that moment to humble yourself in the morning, but find whatever that thing is.

Find the thing that grounds you and reminds you that you aren't simply here to do the things you *want* to do. You are here to do the hard things too.

The annoying things.

The stressful things.

The time-consuming things.

The things for other people that will never bring any benefit to you.

The unnoticed things.

Those are the things that will ultimately pull you closer to your ideal self.

Those are the things that will keep you grounded, humbled, and willing to say no to things that don't add value to your life or others' lives and say yes to the things that do. Maybe you need to set limits on your phone usage every day. Maybe you need to set a reminder to go on a walk, work out, or go for a run. Maybe you need to set out your Bible or journal on your bedside table so that you'll see it soon as you wake up. I don't know what will get your day off to a better start, but I know that it will change the trajectory of how you view yourself if you begin disciplining yourself every morning.

And do the things you say you are going to do. It doesn't matter if no one else knows your plans or knows your goals. It doesn't matter if you shout them to the world or keep them private for only you to know; just do them. When you do so, your standard for what others should live up to will also increase. By doing what you say you're going to do, you automatically and subconsciously start expecting the same from others. By holding yourself accountable, you begin to hold others accountable.

As iron sharpens iron, you become the person challenging your friends, helping them to also see their worth and potential if they would simply follow in your footsteps. If you don't do it for yourself, do it for them. Your friends deserve someone challenging them and having expectations for them. That doesn't mean we won't all fall short and deserve grace, but it means you care enough about them to want them to step into the potential they have. You want to see them have self-respect in whatever area they need it. We females, especially, have to stop settling for less than we deserve simply because we don't believe we deserve to have standards any higher than the next person. You deserve to have high standards for how you are treated, but those should only come if you, yourself, are also being challenged and living up to those same notions.

Discipline gives birth to self-respect, hopefully for not only you but those you surround yourself with as well. Be intentional about choosing your boundaries. Decide before the moment comes where you stand on something. Make yourself do something hard or undesirable every single day—even if that something is simply making your bed. We were meant to work for reward, not sit and wait for it. And not giving into temptation, whatever that might be for you, doesn't come by sitting around and hoping you are strong enough to withstand the tide when it comes for you. It's beginning to take steps now so that once you are in the ocean and a tide comes, you know without a doubt that you'll be standing up after it passes. Put in the work now, be intentional now, so that you won't be shattered and have to build yourself back up later.

FREEDOM IS NEVER
FREE. BUT IT'S ALWAYS
WORTH THE PRICE.

MANDATED ALTRUISM & LEGISLATED MORALITY

There's a reason that we get a choice in this life. There's a reason that we have the option to be intentional or to be lackadaisical with our decision-making.

If you're a believer and follower of Jesus, you'll have already heard and understand how important free will is. Without choice, there would be no love.

Dictatorship is not love. You can't force someone in to love, or it ceases to be love. We get the choice to follow Jesus in this life because if we didn't have the choice, there would be no way for us to let love in. The sacrifice made on the cross would be in vain, and there would be no need for an atonement for our sins.

The reason Jesus's sacrifice made each one of us whole is because it was done out of and specifically for love. Now we get to accept that gift in love and choose to reciprocate it back by believing and allowing transformation in our lives. How do we do this? We permit His purpose to be fulfilled through us.

We would be incapable of loving God without the free will to choose to love him; therefore, he allows it. And with him allowing us to have free will, we also have the choice to accept or deny

Him. We have the choice to make right or wrong decisions, go down paths that lead to despair or lead to abundance. We get to choose what we believe, when we believe it, and give a reason as to why we believe it. We get to say yes, no, or—rarely—maybe.

Without free will in the equation, we are nothing more than anatomical robots carrying out our pre-determined purpose. And hey, maybe that wouldn't be half bad. But then again, would you rather be guaranteed food, water, and shelter but held down by shackles and chains behind bars? Or would you rather experience freedom with the chance at food, water, and shelter? One of these options guarantees comfort but denies freedom, and the other guarantees freedom while still giving a chance at comfort. It reminds me of a scene in *The Last Battle* where C.S. Lewis writes:

"No, no, no," howled the Beasts. "It can't be true. Aslan would never sell us into slavery to the King of Calormen."

"None of that! Hold your noise!" said the Ape with a snarl. "Who said anything about slavery? You won't be slaves. You'll be paid—very good wages too. That is to say, your pay will be paid into Aslan's treasury and he will use it all for everybody's good." Then he glanced, and almost winked, at the chief Calormene. The Calormene bowed and replied, in the pompous Calormene way:

"Most sapient Mouthpiece of Aslan, The Tisroc (may-he-live-forever) is wholly of one mind with your lordship in this judicious plan."

"There! You see!" said the Ape. "It's all arranged. And all for your own good. We'll be able, with the money you earn, to make Narnia a country worth living in. There'll be oranges and bananas pouring in—and roads and big cities and schools and offices and whips and muzzles and saddles and cages and kennels and prisons—Oh, everything."

"But we don't want all those things," said an old Bear. "We want to be **free**."

Without a choice, we are no longer independent, individualistic, and unique people. We are each one and the same, trying our best not to step out of line, out of the ordinary, so that our needs will still be met. As C.S. Lewis says (you can tell by this point, I'm a big fan of his), "If you look for truth, you may find comfort in the end; if you look for comfort you will not get either comfort or truth, only soft soap and wishful thinking to begin, and in the end, despair."

The evidence of the importance of choices goes deeper and further than a theological debate. Each day, our choices impact us and hold us to a standard. We are allowed to fail, succeed, and land somewhere in between because of our choices. We get to alter our personal realities, and the majority of the time, our choices alter the realities of others.

This brings me to the title of the chapter: Mandated Altruism & Legislated Morality

The problem with forcing people to give, forcing people to be altruistic, is that you form a paradox in which that person can no longer be altruistic.

Just like love, altruism can only be created through choice. By forcing someone to give more money, to serve more, to care more about the overall well-being of others, you are stripping away that person's freedoms to do so, hence hindering altruism altogether and leaving nothing more than a duty to be fulfilled. Even though some of our tax money is used for great things, we rarely feel the joy and fulfillment of giving since the money is taken from us rather than us giving by choice.

Now, this is not to say we should be against all "duties," as we already discussed in a previous chapter the importance of discipline and practicing obedience. In addition to that, governments choosing to take a percentage from everyone to spur the development of basic necessities of a functioning society is also not a bad thing. We all use the roads, we all appreciate education, but once every aspect of our generosity becomes solely an act of mandated altruism, we lose the altruism itself and, in that, we lose the benefits a person reaps from being altruistic.

An article on Zillionist titled "Altruism in the Brain" describes studies that observed the functions of the brain when people were allowed to participate in acts of altruism.

First, the article gives us background on the neuroscience to help us better understand how this works.

The nucleus accumbens is a region in the brain that plays an important role in the brain's rewards circuit. Study shows that when participants donated money, the activity in the nucleus accumbens spiked. This brain region is activated by dopamine (which promotes desire) and serotonin (which promotes inhibition and satiety). When we perform reward-related behavior, like eating great food, this leads to an increase in dopamine levels in the nucleus accumbens. As a result, we do not only feel good but also want to do it again!

Now for the results:

Altruistic behavior does not only have an effect on dopamine but also on endorphins and oxytocin. Giving promotes the release of endorphins in the brain, producing that great feeling known as the "helper's high." Oxytocin, also known as the "cuddle hormone," plays a major role in social interaction. Oxytocin is also released when we give. This in turn leads to a reduction of social fears and increased social bonding.

I wish I could say I was surprised by these results, but anyone who has intentionally sought out a place to serve or a way to give, or has pursued the challenge of improving someone else's life in any way, can say they have felt the rush of satisfaction and pure joy the article is describing.

The science adds up to the feeling.

And this goes to show the importance of intentionality. There are countless other articles out there discussing quite the opposite of this one. They discuss how we feel a sense of rebellion when made to do something or simply don't reap the rewards of dopamine, oxytocin, and endorphins being resurged like we do when we have the *choice* to give or help someone. Having the choice to give versus being made to give has quite the opposite effect.

When our choices are taken away, part of our will to live is taken away. We lose our ability to be intentional with our actions. When our ability to be intentional is taken away, we are left unable to transform, carrying the weight of who we currently are rather than throwing that off to chase after who we desire to be.

"Give me liberty, or give me death" wasn't a sentence to be taken lightly when Patrick Henry uttered it back in 1775, and it should still ring victorious in our minds today. Mandated altruism ceases to be altruism at all. By stripping down our choices, our right to intentionally choose to help someone, we are left questioning whether if we had the choice, we would have ever helped that person to begin with. We are left without a clear picture of who we are because all we know is who we are being made to be.

Without choice, introspection becomes a guessing game and a hoping game. We are guessing at what choices we would make if we could and hoping those choices would be the right ones.

This cold, dark world already causes us grief, heartache, and adversity beyond what we think we can bear. By mandating altruism, by making people give more, we are once again adding to the layer of stone around our hearts, making it impossible to see the good we are capable of doing—the impact we are able to make on people's lives through having a servant's heart. You can call it idealistic, but the proof is in the data. The proof is in our biology, our makeup. We are a people encouraged and stimulated by purpose, and our purpose is heightened when we can choose to give freely to those we believe need it. We are created to wrestle with how much we think we can give.

The irony in giving is that when people have a choice, they tend to give more. When people are required to be altruistic, they tend to give the bare minimum.

The answer is not "power to the administrators, the rulers, the dictators, the socialists"; it's "power to the people." The power we have as human beings to love those around us is so much greater than we allow ourselves to see. Our clouded ideas about ourselves seep into our ideas of who our neighbors are as well.

Without choice, we don't have introspection.

Without introspection, we don't know who we are or how good we can be.

Without knowing how good we are capable of being, we assume less of ourselves and less of our neighbors because we are all doing the minimum, doing our duties and being stripped from our preferences.

Secondly, most of us have heard someone at some point say, "You can't legislate morality." I would have to agree with Martin Luther King, Jr. when he says, "Morality cannot be legislated, but behavior can be regulated. Judicial decrees may not change the heart, but they can restrain the heartless."

My question is, if we are restraining the heartless, why would we also choose, by mandating altruism, to restrain the heart-filled? As previously mentioned, taking away the decision to do good is nothing more than putting a glass ceiling over those who would be willing to give more if they had the choice to begin with. Just as we cannot expect legislating morality to cure people's inability to have compassion for others, mandating altruism will also not enhance people's ability to have compassion and care for the well-being of others.

In the end, it's a heart that needs to be fixed and fine-tuned towards the needs of others, not a monetary problem where dollars are the primary solution. The intention behind the heart matters. Giving without that intention is only scratching the surface of humanity's selfishly rooted problem.

Having the right to be intentional, to choose between right and wrong, to choose where we invest our time, how much we invest our time, when we give, who we give to, how much we give, all of these things are pivotal to allowing us to wrestle out the inner workings of our heart. You can't change what you don't know. And you can't know your true heart without having a choice to make.

Some of you may be thinking that this is putting a lot of trust in humanity to make the right choices, to put pressure on people to help others. That's because, without it, those people may not survive, or at least may not have as comfortable of a life as they would with guaranteed provision.

This is when I discuss the unpopular concept of "picking oneself up by the bootstraps."

I've only discussed the tip of the iceberg as to why our liberties, choices, and freedoms are not just important but imperative for inward transformation. There are countless other books, statistics, personal antidotes, and economic explanations as to why we need them ever so desperately.

As I've stated before, in the United States, we are taken care of to a certain extent by the tax dollars we give for shared services, international protection, and other programs already created to help ourselves or our fellow neighbors. By regulating anything more, by mandating anything more, we are taking on more duties and responsibilities for others' benefit without reaping any altruistic reward for ourselves and also without pushing those on the receiving end closer to social responsibility—another invigorating reward that gives this life purpose.

The reason many of us in this day and age fail to see the joys of life, the many blessings we have been given, the potential we have, the dreams inside of us, is because we are too focused on being the victim. We can't fathom what it would look like to become the victor.

We are content with the self-pity as well as the responsibility being taken off of us and put on the backs of others to make our lives a bit easier. We are content with the attention we receive, not by working hard to overcome our circumstances, but by screaming out to others that we have been given an unfair disadvantage and it's everyone else's job to fix it.

We see our hardships, our trials, the unfairness in our lives, and the things that make us different from others or even disadvantaged. Instead of overcoming those things, instead of conquering them, we wallow and beg at the coattails of others to help make our lives a little bit better. We are once again begging for scraps of negative attention instead of proudly creating positive attention ourselves by overcoming our circumstances.

You are not a victim.

If the holocaust survivors like Viktor Frankl or Corrie Ten Boom do not call themselves victims, you also are not a victim.

If Jesus Christ didn't call himself a victim, you are not a victim.

This life isn't fair. When sin crept in, it was never meant from that day forward to be fair. Free will causes this life to be anything but fair. Some of us have it easier than others, but no one escapes this world alive. No one escapes this world without losing someone they care about. No one walks through this life without trials and hardship and times when they wonder if they can muster up the courage to continue on. But you get to choose if you are going to let your circumstances determine your attitude and determine how much you believe you are "owed" by those around you.

You get to choose if your life is meaningful enough, if the lives of those around you are meaningful enough, for you to do your part. Social responsibility doesn't take away from you; it gives you something to live for that's greater than yourself. We will never gain the satisfaction of living a purposeful life if we are constantly begging from others rather than seeing what it's like ourselves to take care of someone.

By all of us choosing to take on responsibility, we will no longer need mandated altruism. People will be waiting in lines to volunteer, giving their last dime to someone who has less than they do, fearlessly stepping out to speak about things they've overcome, begging to help others who have walked through similar hardships as them.

But someone has to pave the way first. Someone has to be the first to declare themselves the victor in a situation where most would call them the victim.

I hope that whatever situation you have fought through, it will be you. I hope you will be one of the brave ones who see their lives as Russian novelist Fyodor Dostoevsky did when he said, "There is only one thing that I dread: not to be worthy of my sufferings."

What an honor to suffer well. What an honor to be entrusted with such a hardship as the one you have experienced. What an honor to have beaten the odds, to stand up and take responsibility for making something of your life without needing pity or help from others.

You are victorious.

You are not a victim.

And now I hope you understand why intentionality is only possible if we have a choice. And with our choices, we may succeed or fail, but at least we are allowed to fight.

Freedom is never free.

But it's always worth the price.

PART OF FINDING OUR
PURPOSE IS HAVING BIG
ENOUGH DREAMS TO
DISCOVER IT. DREAM BIGGER
AND DREAM BETTER,
BECAUSE RIGHT NOW, NOT
EVEN YOU KNOW WHAT
YOU'RE CAPABLE OF.

YOUR DREAMS AREN'T
BIG ENOUGH

One of the questions I get asked the most is, "How do you travel so much?" I used to dream of how awesome it would be to consider myself a "world traveler." My family loves to travel now, but growing up, we couldn't afford to go very far, so we settled on vacations in South Carolina (which to this day holds such a special place in my heart). I remember feeling so insecure once in college when I was sitting in a class, and the professor made us go around the room and announce our favorite country that we had ever been to. Luckily my family and I had all just gone out of the country together for the first time the year prior, so I had something to say. (We went to Mexico, in case you were wondering.) I listened as the rest of the class named countries I had dreamt of going to. Fellow twenty-something-year-olds had been to countries all over Asia, Africa, Europe; it felt like I was the only one who had only one option to pick from and that one option still being in North America.

It seems that traveling is one of those things you don't really know you enjoy until you get out and do it. Until you leave your comfort zone of the United States, or wherever your home base is, you don't understand the whimsy, the thrill, and the pure magic of traveling to a place so different from home. Maybe I was different, or maybe everyone dreams of going places far and wide, but in that moment in class hearing everyone talk about their favorite places around the world, I realized that one day that would be me too. I didn't know how it would happen or who I would go with, or how I would even pay for it, but I knew I was destined to adventure farther than most and more frequently than most.

Fast forward to that following Christmas break, and the guy I was dating at the time had asked me to go to Europe with him and his family. We would be spending my birthday and Christmas in Europe, and I was so nervous but excited to visit seven countries over the course of that trip. To be honest with you, I think I was in such shock at how different that side of the world is. I observed every detail. From the way they dressed, what they ate, to how they spoke, to how they interacted with one another, I was so inquisitive. I was mesmerized by how tiny the cars were, how narrow the streets were. I couldn't believe how easy it was to drive from one country to another in a day's time and the next country be so drastically different from the last. Luckily, the person I was dating was well versed in travel and had so much to teach me along the way. What a learning experience it was. To this day, I know my love for travel was ignited because of how eye-opening that trip was.

Following that trip, I was able to visit a few more places with him as well as with my family. From Jamaica to South Africa, I was captivated more and more with every new place, new culture, and new adventure.

Following the end of that relationship, I had a lot of time to intimately ask myself what vices I would choose to help me turn the page and start my new chapter alone. It didn't take me long to vote out all of the other options, and I subconsciously decided my vice of choice would be travel. Most people would have called it running from my problems, but I just called it surrendering to the least unhealthy vice I could think of. I have journal entry upon journal entry from that time period voicing how concerned I was that I would end up wasting the heartbreak or putting those emotions into the wrong activities or, just as scary, no activity at all. I wanted to make something beautiful out of this grief. Traveling and adrenaline was always our thing. We went to more countries together and had more adventurous, adrenaline-filled experiences together than most married couples have in a lifetime. I wanted to show myself that even though that chapter of my life had closed, I could still hold onto those passions and still give them the attention that they deserved. Even though I felt like I had lost it all, I could still hold tight to the few passions that made me feel okay again, and traveling was one of those.

This chapter isn't supposed to be primarily about travel; it's supposed to be about our dreams. However, I wouldn't be giving this dream of mine the backbone it deserves without the proper backstory. So after that chapter of my life closed, I began what I would call either a quarter-life crisis or a journey of *true* self-discovery, the latter sounding much better. I began to see once again the things that ignited my spirits. When you are at the lowest point, emotionally, that you've ever been at, it's quite easy to pick out those few things that raise your spirits. I was motivated more than ever not to waste this pain and brokenness; I wanted to see the rawest version of myself and ask her who she was when there was nothing left. I did this, and what I saw was someone too afraid to dream big because either:

1. It didn't seem possible
2. The chances of failure were too high

or

3. I spent more time focusing on small dreams that were more "achievable."

This third point stuck with me and irritated me day in and day out. "What are my dreams?" I would ask myself.

My answers were pretty typical:

- Have a family one day
- Have a successful career
- Travel the world
- Get a dog [I really wanted a dog]
- Go back to art school
- Love people and love Jesus better

Those were basically my "dreams." Now, I'm not saying those aren't great aspirations, but those aren't big enough to call dreams.

More importantly, it's not that they simply aren't big enough, but they also aren't intentional enough.

One thing working in corporate business has taught me is that quantification and directness are important. I am constantly in the mindset of quantifying the value I am adding to my company. I've learned that if you want to impress people, "I helped improve our Walmart business" doesn't do you nearly as much justice as "I increased sales revenue with our Walmart business by 30 percent over the last fiscal year. I did this by gaining distribution and increasing our margins on e-commerce by 12 percent with reduced shipping costs." That last statement goes a long way to prove your value and show your peers what you are actually doing to better the business. It's the same with your personal life. "Having a successful career" is easy to achieve when there isn't a clear goal in mind. What does "successful" even mean? It's different for everyone depending on your circumstances.

So I decided to start narrowing down what I wanted. I decided to start intentionally writing down my goals, and in a way that I could either truly mark them off as achieved or not yet achieved. I began categorizing short-term goals, long-term goals, and the in-between steps that would help me achieve them. Instead of "have a successful career," my short-term goal changed to "get a promotion within the first year and a half of being in my current position." I've been with my company a year and four months now, and last month I had a conversation with my manager about my future and decided it was the right time to ask for the promotion. Instead of "go back to art school," my dream changed to "become a professional sculptor" and the in-between goal to help me get there is now, "go back to art school within the next eight years and graduate with my MFA in sculpture."

I began to get specific with my dreams which led me to get excited about them again. I could see how the next steps were laid out in front of me, and they were finally tangible. "Your dreams aren't big enough" doesn't have a "one size fits all" baseline. YOUR dreams aren't big enough for YOU; other people's accomplishments and goals have nothing to do with it.

Up until me, there had only been one person in my family who had graduated from college. That one other person happens to be my Nana, so there was a large gap between me and her. No blood-related aunts, uncles, parents, grandparents, or great grandparents had gone to college except for my Nana and soon to be me. That said, many of my college friends were living out a three- or four-generational legacy by attending the same university as their siblings, parents, and grandparents.

Many of my friends knew exactly what to expect and had known they were going to college since they were in middle school. They had visited their parents' alma maters, had visited siblings currently in college, and most of them already had a savings account set aside for their own college tuition. I, on the other hand, never really thought about it until high school. My parents were always pushing me to do my best in school, but I was hard enough on myself that they didn't have to discipline me too much; I was that annoying type for whom B's weren't allowed.

So the "college talk" never really happened. I remember talking

more with my parents about what scholarship for basketball I would
try to get, so maybe it just went unsaid that I wanted to pursue a
college degree. Nonetheless, I never felt pressure around it like
most kids my age did. I just felt supported.

When I decided my senior year that I wasn't going to play
college basketball, that I just wanted to focus on academics in
college, it was such a surreal experience going to tour any college
campus that I was interested in with my parents. I remember loving
every second of it because this wasn't just my first time doing
something like this; it was theirs too.

So for me, graduating top of my class at university and becoming
a doctor wasn't my "big dream." Simply going to college at the
time was my big dream. It might not have been big to some of my
peers I would later meet, but it was huge for me. Not to mention,
I knew I would be taking a huge risk by getting into a substantial
amount of debt to attend college.

My point is that your dreams shouldn't be compared to someone
else's, they should be compared to what YOU want to accomplish
in life. The awesome thing about my story is that being a first-generation college student, I got into my dream school, the University
of Kentucky, without having a clue of what I wanted to do. My
first year was extremely tough, and if I hadn't taken AP (Advanced
Placement) classes in high school, I don't think I would have
been prepared enough to make it. But I pushed through, adjusted
my study habits, became more disciplined than ever before, and
decided to adjust my dreams once again. I then decided I didn't
just want to graduate with any degree. I wanted to graduate with

a challenging degree that not just anyone could get, so I chose Economics. I did research and found out that only 14 percent of economists in the world are women and that I would be among the smallest graduating class within the Business and Economics school at the University of Kentucky. To me, at the time, I assumed that meant it would be pretty tough. Continuing throughout those four years I even decided to pick up an art studio minor as well as an international business minor. My dream of "going to college" didn't seem as big anymore now that my eyes were set on bigger and more challenging things within that same realm.

Too often, I see people decide on a goal that is either easily accomplished or, conversely, decide on a difficult goal, but never dreaming bigger once they have achieved it. Our skills change, our mindset changes, our life circumstances change for better and for worse. We have to continue to re-evaluate our dreams and what steps we need to be taking to get there. If I had stopped with "going to college" being my dream, I wouldn't have the career I have now. If I hadn't intentionally decided to do something harder, if I hadn't sacrificed a lot more than I had to simply by going to college, I wouldn't be where I am now—living out a separate dream I had of working at the World Headquarters of a Fortune 1000 company.

I am so grateful for younger Katlyn looking fear in the eyes and saying that she is going to go beyond what anyone expects of her and beyond what she even expects of herself. I am so thankful that she knew her dreams were too small without having done any true introspection to figure it out. I want to reiterate time and time again: your dreams aren't big enough for YOU.

Don't look at someone else's journey and see them doing things beyond your scope of what you want or where you are. Look only at your life and say, "Can I do better? Is this really pushing me? Is this even what *I* want?" Be intentional in chasing your dreams. Make them tangible. If you want to dance on Broadway one day, there are plenty of people who made that a reality, and they didn't do it by wishing and hoping. They did it by putting in work and taking the necessary steps to get there. They hit a million tiny goals before they made their grand dream a reality.

I have quite a few huge dreams, but I can break those down into small segments that I am intentionally pursuing these days.

I told myself I wouldn't lose my passions, hopes, and dreams just because one of them was shattered. I now have that dog I always wanted (and yes, he is the cutest Newfoundland ever). I asked for the promotion and received the absolute best feedback from my manager. I now actually have a new position. I start back graduate school next week. I traveled to Canada, Puerto Rico, Cambodia, and drove the Pacific Coast Highway in California last year alone. This year I've already been to Florida, Texas a few times, Wyoming, Tennessee, Ohio, Montana, Idaho, Portland, and Hawaii. I am doing the dang/damn (you choose) thing.

My dreams are bigger than ever before, but they are also more tangible than ever before. There are people out there chasing dreams to write a *New York Times* bestseller. Down the road, that is mine too. But for now, I just want to claim the title "author" and publish a book that I have poured my heart into. No matter if I crash and burn, if everyone who reads it hates it, if I look back one day and laugh at my effort, I don't care. This is my dream now, and I know I will continue to grow and transform into bigger dreams as this one comes to a close.

To become confident people, we have to know our purpose. Part of finding our purpose is having big enough dreams to discover it. Dream bigger and dream better, because right now, not even you know what you're capable of.

PART IV

Confidence

WE'RE CONSTANTLY
WORKING FOR THE
APPROVAL OF OTHERS THAT
SOMETIMES I WONDER IF
HALF OF US EVEN REALLY
LIKE OURSELVES.

RIPE ORANGES

I don't know what it was that shattered your confidence. Or for some of you, I don't know what chain of events shattered your confidence, but I do know that you weren't created to live in guilt or shame or constant insecurity. I know you weren't put on this earth to spend each day feeling as if you aren't good enough to be loved, to achieve your dreams, or to find your purpose.

Whether you believe in the same God I do or something else, I can't imagine a supernatural creator of the universe putting you here by chance just so that you can live in misery day in and day out. So what was it? I'm not a therapist or a counselor, but I think the thing we can both agree on is that most people tend to scratch the surface of their problems only enough to find a short-term fix instead of digging down to the root of what hurt them and pulling it up so that nothing else remains. So think about it, what caused you to lose the love for yourself you once had? Kids don't lie to their parents for no reason. Kids lie because they believe the repercussions for what they did will hurt them more than lying for the sake of getting out of it. Lying is worth "saving face" if it means they:

1. Don't get in trouble

and

2. Don't disappoint their parents.

Their overall well-being is worth more to them than the risk they're taking of getting caught in a lie. They believe themselves to be valuable and don't want anyone else to think otherwise. So at some point, whether you were a child or much older, when was it that you lost that self-favoring attitude? I'm not saying adults don't lie as well, but adults lie for much more complicated and complex reasons than children.

If it helps, I'll tell my story.

I grew up thinking I would take on the world one day. (See, even just as I was typing, I initially put "could" but remembered that my younger self would have said that I WOULD take on the world one day. I'm still working on the confidence thing myself.) Looking back, I don't think I was arrogant. I just loved who I was and knew I was capable of doing big things. I think most kids have big dreams, another piece of evidence that once upon a time, you believed in yourself much more than you might now. Think back to the first day of first grade or whenever that was when your teacher made you write down what you wanted to be when you grew up. I remember so many kids in my class saying, "astronaut, veterinarian, President of the United States, doctor, teacher, artist, police officer," and so many other amazing careers that I doubt many of them decided they had the ability to pursue once they got older.

As I grew up, I noticed how I always wanted to be the protector for others, back to my Enneagram 8 traits. So I carried myself well, I took on leadership roles, I wanted to be the best role model to others, I never drank alcohol (literally not until I was almost twenty-three), I didn't cuss, I didn't do a lot of the things people my age were doing because I believed I was capable of inspiring others by doing this. Fast forward to college, not much changed besides meeting many more people, finding new hobbies, passions, and trying to be disciplined with all things in life. The big thing that did change was I started dating someone halfway through my junior year.

I'll skip the details of the relationship, but overall, it was great. Looking back now, of course, I see things I would have changed but to be honest, those things are probably just because I'm older now and see life a little differently. However, back then, I was genuinely happy, challenged, encouraged, inspired, and so full of joy in the relationship. Things weren't always perfect, but the guy I was with was so much like myself at the time that arguing just didn't happen much. For two years of my life I was showered with love and admiration for parts of who I was. I was given compliments on so many aspects of who I was, and to this day, I'm thankful that my college dating experience primarily created great memories.

However, what I didn't learn until long after the relationship ended is that if we aren't careful, when we love someone deeply, we might begin only loving the parts of ourselves that person loves. Instead of loving the parts that we truly love and are proud of, we begin to only be satisfied and content with the parts of ourselves that he (or she) is satisfied with. For someone who had so much confidence and ambition before and during the relationship, once it was over, I found myself scavenging to find pieces of myself I felt were good enough. All of those parts that were once so appreciated by the person who meant the most to me were now useless and no longer desired.

Whether it was the way I looked, my mind, my thoughtfulness, my ambition, my love for the outdoors, my spirituality, my work ethic, whatever it was, it no longer suited that person. For the record, I didn't understand any of this at first. It wasn't until much later that I realized the woman who was known for being confident, inspiring, and even a little bit intimidating had been not just fooling others, but undoubtedly fooling herself. It wasn't that I consciously knew I was only loving who I was because the person I loved and valued the most was loving those parts about me. It was something I subconsciously held for who knows how long.

And let's be honest, there's nothing wrong with wanting to impress those you care about. There's nothing wrong with wanting to be the best you can be, to inspire those around you, or to want to be well-versed in anything and everything so that you can have common ground with more people. That should be our goal in a relationship—to be our best version of ourselves so that we will be able to challenge, inspire, and encourage the other person to be their best self as well. But once we begin only being proud of or valuing the parts of us the other person values, we've become lost in a cycle of living up to the next expectation of *their* desires, not our own. And this isn't something your girlfriend or boyfriend or spouse can fix for you or something you can blame on an ex-girlfriend, ex-boyfriend, or ex-spouse. This is something that even the most strong and resolute individuals can succumb to because the slippery slope of approval is so easy to find ourselves on in this life.

Looking back, I never realized this about myself because we enjoyed and loved almost all of the same things. We appreciated the same things about one another. I had no idea that when I stopped receiving that appreciation, I would be left with no love for those things, much less any other aspects of myself that I used to love.

It took me a long time not only to see this but also to begin the process of learning who I was again and loving her—loving her so much that anyone could come or go, and I would still be left standing in front of the mirror, smiling just the same.

As I was reflecting on this journey, I remembered a post I made on social media that gives a little more practicality to how you can become more attuned to the soul of the person you should love the most: you.

I hope you all are still finding freedom in the midst of the crazy times we are living in.

A few months ago when quarantine/social distancing [referencing the Coronavirus Pandemic] first started, I told myself I wanted to spend more time alone and really learn new things about me.

So I did.

I made art. I wrote. I read. I cooked. I baked. I gardened. I taught myself how to longboard. I taught myself how to whistle (finally). I went fishing. I worked out. I shot guns. I stargazed. I went swimming. And I spent many days and nights doing things alone and learning about myself, trying new things, and just letting myself wander wherever I wanted.

And turns out... I'm not that bad!

I feel like we spend our lives so busy and preoccupied that we never get to sit down by ourselves and learn who we really are. There are so many passions, hobbies, and people out there that you would ADORE... You just haven't met them yet. And you don't slow down enough to even get the chance.

We're constantly working for the approval of others that sometimes I wonder if half of us even really like ourselves.

Turns out the Katlyn I like most is the one with messy hair, no makeup on, wood stain on her hands, no shoes, who has been working on a sculpture all day, dancing to her favorite music, with a paintbrush behind her ear.

Or the one who checks on her plants in the morning with her cup of tea in hand, eager to see if the strawberry blooms have finally sprouted.

Those are the versions of me I haven't seen in a while, and others I have never met until the last few

months. Hobbies I never knew I had. Passions I had
forgotten. Dreams that had been pushed to the back
of my mind were finally alone enough to come back
knocking at the front door... ready to be greeted again.

If you haven't yet, spend some more time alone this
season. You'll be glad you did.

Maybe this is something we all have to learn on our own. Still,
I hope by hearing my story, someone out there can realize sooner
rather than later that their confidence in themselves will either
propel them into a place of joy and a dream-chasing mentality,
or it will keep them where they feel like they are drowning in
insecurity and brokenness. I can promise you now that you won't
look back one day and wish you had hated more things about
yourself. One day you're going to look back and wish you had
believed in yourself a little more and valued what *you* thought of
yourself a lot more than what others thought of you.

The last thing I want to say is, don't be afraid to do things
alone. As I mentioned in my post above, I spent a lot of time
alone during the first few months of the pandemic, and I found so
much freedom during that season. I did many things alone; I even
occasionally went to restaurants by myself. As crazy as it sounds,
I truly believe that when we begin taking ourselves out without
other people to impress, entertain, or compromise with, we begin
to see the truest and most raw version of ourselves.

We finally get to really know what [your name] would do if
she/he had no obligations.

We get to see how [your name] wants to dress or how long he/ she wants to sit in a coffee shop and read a book.

We get to sit and listen to ourselves think and observe and learn how our brains process information, because it is different for each of us. I found myself asking questions I had never thought to ask before. I saw my mind ache for a creative outlet again; it was almost as if I was so busy before that I had never slowed down enough to hear my soul's cry for creativity. I began not to care what anyone else around me thought. I was solely driven to learn something new about myself each day. I slowly became my own friend again.

In the beginning, it was intimidating and felt a little uncomfortable, to be honest, but the longer I pushed through, the more I loved the person I was spending the most time with again. I began to see those parts of my character, my mind, my desires in a new light again, and after a long, hard battle of pretending to appreciate them, I truly did this time.

The truth I held was no longer "I'm not good enough." My truth was no longer based on what someone else thought. Now, the truth I held was, "I am good enough because I am proud of the woman in this body." Actually, more than that, I *love* the woman in this body. She is smarter than I ever knew; her mind is my favorite thing about her. She is athletic and can be disciplined with her health and wellness if she tries. She is funny (to herself, and that's all that matters). She is adventurous and spontaneous and has a work ethic like no one I've seen. She is inquisitive and can never ask enough questions. She is creative and truly has the hands of an artist. She empowers others to chase their dreams. She is a good friend and is loyal to the core. She is beautiful; whether anyone else thinks so or not, she simply *is*.

The more time I spent with myself, the more I started believing those things whole-heartedly. Not because I was hearing them from someone else, but because I was witnessing them with my own two eyes. I never thought I would need to "re-learn to love myself," but I've realized the things in life you never thought you'd have to do are likely the ones you'll end up doing.

Love yourself for the right reasons, the real reasons, and challenge yourself to be better for the right reasons as well. One day life will come and try to knock you down, and the reality of who you are is what will make you stand tall on the ground of confidence. Let no one know your flaws and your strengths better than you do, and let no one's love or hate for them hold more weight than yours does.

Because, as my mom used to tell me when I was a little girl, "You can be the ripest, most beautiful, and sweetest orange in the bunch, but there's always going to be someone who just doesn't like oranges."

THERE IS ALWAYS A
PLENTIFUL HARVEST TO
REAP ON THE GROUNDS
OF COURAGE.

BEWARE OF BEARS

I had just moved into my new house, and I decided to go for a run to explore the area. Summer was slowly turning into fall, and the air in the afternoon began to get a little crisper by the day. As I was running, I saw a huge walking/bike trail off the road that was canopied by enormous trees that looked like a hidden forest (I'm a sucker for some big trees, and these kinds of trees are not common where I live). So I began veering off in that direction, and as I made my way onto the trail, I saw an elderly couple accompanied by two young boys that looked like they were their grandchildren. As I approached them from behind, I slowed down and began to walk a short distance from them. Afraid they might say something to me and I would not hear, I turned my music down as I passed them, but they returned only a smile at me. I smiled back, but before I turned my music back up, I couldn't help but see that one of the little boys looked so afraid. He was taking slow steps into the trail, and his presupposed grandparents were trying to coax him in by saying that there was nothing to be afraid of. I turned back at him, and he said, "but what if there are bears in here?" Immediately the grandpa laughed and said, "We're in Lexington, Kentucky; there are no bears here." I saw the little boy sigh in relief. Comfort washed over his face, but right after that, what looked to be his twin brother (if not younger brother as he was even smaller) said with excitement and eagerness in his voice, "But there might be bears, right? Could there *maybe* be bears in here?" This little boy desperately wanted his grandpa to say yes, but he just laughed once again and told him that bears didn't live in places like this. I couldn't help but laugh myself at the boy and admire his courage. I watched him a little further as he walked onto the trail, proudly in front, leading his family into the (almost dark now) woods. He had no fear in the world.

I couldn't shake the thought of these two little boys the rest of my run.

How many times am I the first boy, and how many times am I his brother?

How often am I afraid to walk into a place so beautiful because I can't seem to just get right around the corner?

How many places full of mystery have I not been willing to go to, metaphorically and even physically, because I am afraid of what I might find?

How often am I hesitant to get uncomfortable for a second, even if it means seeing something marvelous for the first time?

How often do I need to be pushed instead of being the leader of the group guiding everyone else safely into the unknown?

Ultimately, both boys walked into the woods, but one walked in with confidence, and one walked in scared. Even though I prefer to be like the second boy, I still admire the first who walked in, even scared.

I feel like we have two parts of our confidence to build, and some of us only hover around one of them instead of pushing through into the second. It's like that phrase you've heard over and over, "Go the extra mile." The reason we don't have people chasing their dreams, changing the world, and using their gifts in miraculous ways is that we only have people going halfway. Once we begin to get a little uncomfortable, we stop.

Pastor Levi Lusko of Fresh Life Church gives this example: "Give till it hurts. You'll know once you're giving enough to others because the last bit of it will be tough to let go of; it'll hurt."

I love this example as so many of us stay within the confinements of our comfort zone. When we are asked or guided to go farther than that, we retreat and justify why we can't. Just that small bit of advice from Levi Lusko has changed the way I give now. I've begun giving what I'm comfortable with each month and then adding a little more. It hurts, but it's so invigorating knowing that I'm getting out of my comfort zone and trusting God to use me and my finances in big ways—bigger than what I even feel comfortable with.

Part 1 of building our confidence: doing things scared.

Part 2 of building our confidence: learning to do things fearless.

As I said, I believe that so many of us are only living halfway into the confident beings we were created to be. Some of us aren't even living that much, but I would dare to say that half of us reading this book are fierce in one way or another and have freely chosen in their lives to do certain things even though we were scared. In all honesty, I'm writing this book entirely scared. I actually gave up on it once because of how intimidated I was and how I didn't believe I was good enough or equipped enough to finish it.

Here is some evidence from my social media:

Part 1 | Big Announcement

It was mid-July of 2019, and I was sitting by the pool at my apartment complex when I felt this supernatural pull to run into my house and start writing. If you know me, you know I'm a thinker, and I'm not a fan of verbalizing those thoughts in any way. And at that moment, it was almost as if God (or something in my head) inaudibly yelled at me and said, "Go start writing this stuff down. Everything you're thinking. I want you to write a book."

For the record, I've not ever had a deep desire to be an author. Of course, like most people, I've always thought it would be incredible, but I have never taken any steps to be able to pursue something like that. I'm much more confident in math, data analytics, and statistics than I'll ever be at English or literature.

Back to the story: so I immediately got up, went back to my apartment, and started writing an outline of what I wanted this "book" to be all about. I bought books on "How To Write A Best-Selling Novel" and started reading like never before (it's hard to be a successful writer if you're not an avid reader).

I wrote and wrote and wrote and wrote. On planes. On the beach. In the mountains. Overseas. In my room. On my balcony. In the kitchen. Everywhere.

And then I got stuck. Writing a book is freaking hard by the way... Especially when you're 23 and have no idea what the heck you're doing. So I saw myself starting to write less and less, and before I knew it, I was just convinced that I wasn't good enough to be a writer. That I was too young. Not enough life experience. Not able to articulate my thoughts as well as I thought. Lacking a dense vocabulary to pull from. Etc. Etc.

So I gave up.

Part 2 | Big Announcement

Fast forward a few months, and I was on a boat in the middle of the ocean, sitting at the very front with my feet dangling off, riding into the sunset (ya, it was as magical as it sounds).

I was sitting there looking out into the vast ocean and began thinking how crazy different my life looks now compared to what I thought it would look like a year ago. I thought to myself, "I have no idea where I'm going or what I'm even doing for that matter when I used to have everything planned out." I looked up to the sky and, under my breath, said to God, "What now?? What do you want from me?" & at that moment, a wave crashed in front of us and completely soaked me from the waist down.

I laughed it off and took that as a sign from God to 1. Relax. and 2. Think about what he has asked me for that I haven't done.

And the first thing to come to my mind was, "I've asked you to do one thing, and you haven't done it, to write the book."

So here I am now, jumping back on the journey of becoming a writer. I'm doing it scared and intimidated, but I'm doing it. Who knows if it will be self-published or a NYTBS or if it'll be printed at Staples and bound together by me with some glue and scissors... But regardless, I'm doing it.

This post is holding me accountable because, as my friend Nina says, "We are Dream Doers." I'm tired of hearing people say their dreams but never take steps toward doing them. I'm tired of seeing people with calls from the Lord or passions buried deep within that they never tap into due to fear. Be a dreamer, but more importantly, BE A DO-ER.

Katlyn A. Davis - Author In The Making
What about you?

If you're reading this, I must have succeeded.
If I had never picked myself up after I felt the initial months

of defeat, this dream of mine or maybe even God's dream for me would have never happened. My personality struggles deeply with defeat. I struggle with anything that I know I might fail at. Anything that could potentially "win" over me, I run away from and go fight a battle I know I'm going to win. The older I've gotten, the more I've learned how horrible of a mindset this is to have. If I'm never challenging my mind, body, and spirit to take on more than I think I can stand, I'll never experience any kind of breakthroughs or growth that God has for me behind the next door.

I used to think doing anything that scared me was out of the picture. If I'm going to be afraid, I might as well not do it. I somehow had this false idea that doing things when scared was synonymous with doing things "halfway," when those are two completely different things. Since I am writing this book with so much intimidation and fear, I'm going all in and working twice as hard to be sure it's something I will be proud of once publishing time comes. There is always a plentiful harvest to reap on the grounds of courage. Because as I've said before, one can never be courageous unless he/she was once scared. We don't become brave when attacking things we weren't scared of in the first place.

We become brave, heroic, courageous, and dauntless when we are put in an uncomfortable situation and choose to step into the woods (possibly filled with bears) even if it means being coerced and encouraged to get there. Nonetheless, we stepped in when many others didn't have the courage to.

But don't stop here. Do things scared, but *learn* to do things fearless.

I have recently become what some may call a "wine snob." Kidding, I don't like the term "snob," but over the last year or so, I have fallen in love with everything about wine. First off, who doesn't love grapes? But secondly, the harvest, the process, the fermentation, the community in wine country, the vineyards, everything about the wine-making process, I am so intrigued by. I've become a wine club member at a local winery and have even started working part-time for another winery in town just so that I can continue to be around it and soak up everything I can learn about wine-making. People who knew me a year ago would have laughed if they heard this. I was not the biggest fan of wine. Sweet or dry, red or white; honestly, none of it was for me. But as most wine connoisseurs know, it's something that grows on you over time.

It's the same for bourbon. I live in the state where 95 percent of the world's bourbon is produced; it's everywhere you go in Kentucky but especially Lexington. I live thirty minutes from the bourbon trails (if you don't know what that is, google it or even better, come see it for yourself), and I swore I would never like the taste of bourbon, but here I am after six years of living in Kentucky, finally enjoying and really loving the taste of bourbon. Some things just take time to grow on you.

And I'm not saying either of these two things are for everyone. Some things might not grow on you. I don't see myself ever liking coffee. Still, the moral of the story is that some things have to be pursued or at least given time before they become something you're comfortable with or something you enjoy. I never made myself try bourbon or wine. I just saw myself trying different kinds over time, and before I knew it, my mind had changed, and I was finding out about another part of myself that I never knew existed. I would go as far as saying that most people probably aren't the biggest fan of either drink the first time they try it, same with coffee, but the patience, learning, and inquisitiveness makes one continue to try it, and some of us learn to appreciate it. I believe this to be the case with fearlessness.

I don't think fearlessness is something that the majority of us are born with. I think a large chunk of the population, even those who are fairly confident, have hesitations on how far they will go before they begin avoiding risk. Fearlessness has to be learned. Walking into the woods scared is the first step. Walking into the woods fearless is the second.

After I went skydiving, so many people asked me if I'm not scared of heights. I always laughed and said, "Even if I was, I guess I can't say I am now." Fearlessness takes someone who is willing to do things scared over and over and over again, to the point that every next time gets a little easier and a little less intimidating. The risk is high when you've never looked the challenge directly in the eyes. Once you have, time after time, the risk seems to become a little less, and the reward begins to grow more and more. Failing seems detrimental until you've failed numerous times in a row, yet haven't given up, and the most recent time you succeeded. Failing seems detrimental until you finally do what you've always been afraid of, and you actually come out on top. How do we ever expect to gain confidence unless the thing we are trying to accomplish has some risk involved?

There's nothing confidence-boosting about an easy task that anyone can do. I went skydiving, not because heights aren't scary (they are), but because I had faced other challenges scarier and had come out okay—not just okay, invigorated. This was nothing different. I went cage diving with sharks because I had already been skydiving and knew what being fearless felt like, and I wanted that rush again. There are still things in my life I am working on being fearless towards. I have a long way to go and haven't mastered everything, but there are some things I can now take on "headstrong into the storm," to quote my favorite band NeedTo-Breathe. I learned to love adrenaline because I started challenging myself to do uncomfortable things—to ride the big roller coasters when I was little, to go zip-lining, to give that public speech, to go rock-climbing, to go skydiving, to go cage diving with sharks. Do you see the trend here?

I started challenging myself and growing the fearlessness inside of me, and here I am now at twenty-three, ready to take on the next big adrenaline rush, whatever that may be. There are people well beyond my years willing to do much more intimidating and scary things—people who have been on this journey far longer than I have. But there are also people much older than me who haven't even started.

We are all on a journey towards becoming the best versions of ourselves, and I think confidence plays a huge role in that. Whether you're just beginning to do things you're scared of or you're an old pro, keep going. Keep doing the things, even if you have to do them scared. And for those of you who are already there, who are already taking steps to make big decisions, doing life-changing things, keep pushing yourself out of your comfort zone so that one day you'll be taking on life totally fearless. Imagine how unstoppable one would be who has the courage to take on any challenge without giving fear the reins to pull them back in at any given moment. That's the realm where our world-changers, dream-chasers, and difference-makers live, and hopefully, one day you'll reside there too.

I DON'T KNOW IF ANYONE HAS
TOLD YOU, BUT YOU DON'T
HAVE TO BE AN EXPERT ON
EVERYTHING.

UNTITLED 1

I used to think the more involved I was in a situation, the closer up I could see every detail, the clearer everything would become. I used to think that if I became a subject matter expert on something, I would reap perfection. I would tire myself to know the ins and outs of everything I was interested in, just so that I could be prepared for anything that might happen. If I was as close as possible, in every way, how could I miss anything in the fine print?

In relationships, I would check every box to be sure I was covering the grounds so that the only result I would have would be a successful, happy relationship.

In my career, I would try my best to check every box by knowing every detail about an issue when one would arise. I would focus on the minute parts of a complex problem hoping that I wouldn't be caught off guard if the resolution so happened to be found there; I didn't want anyone else to have found it first either.

Today as I walked around Teton Village in Jackson, Wyoming, I couldn't stop staring at the encapsulating mountains that surrounded me. As postcard-esque as you can imagine, they almost looked fake standing off in the distance. I felt like at any moment someone was going to tear down a green screen, and there would be nothing left of them. This last year as I've grown and changed more than any other year of my life, I began changing my habits and rewiring how I process information. Little by little, change came, and I welcomed it but with hesitation.

I've come to realize that sometimes when we try to be perfect, when we try to narrow in on issues that are a part of such a bigger plan, we miss the giant landscape in front of us. We miss the joy of the process, the clarity in the zoomed-out picture, and the beauty in allowing ourselves to be corrected and redirected. I think the reason I was such a good box-checker is because I was afraid to be corrected. I still don't like the thought of someone else having information on something that I don't. Being wrong is such a humbling feeling and, on the negative side, can even seem humiliating if we aren't prepared for it.

I was reminded time after time this week in the Grand Teton National Park how I wouldn't get the best photo or the best vision with my own two eyes if I were too close to the object in front of me. I found myself continuously trying to get closer, and the closer I got, ironically, the less I saw. "Isn't this how I used to pursue life?" I thought to myself.

I wonder how many times I missed the joys of life by focusing on perfection.

I wonder how many times I would have had the confidence to succeed if I'd had a little grace for myself instead of being indescribably hard on myself.

I wonder how many times I tried to meddle in God's business just so that I would reap the reward I thought I deserved for all of my "hard work."

So many times would I say, "I trust you, God" but continue pacing towards the mountains to get a closer look. I'm not sure, but I have this idea that God would just laugh at me every time this would happen. Besides those times when I was wailing and crying, begging Him to show me His way. I think He probably just sat with me during those.

I've come to realize that no matter how hard we plan, no matter how hard we try to eliminate all the risk, sometimes the dice just aren't rolled in our favor. More importantly, I've realized that I can't let those ill-rolled dice come in and wreck my confidence. Granted, there are times when I could have done more to prevent a tornado that came into my life and absolutely smashed everything, but more times than not, life has chosen to take me on a different path—one I didn't want to go on—and it wasn't my fault.

If we are so closely zoomed in on every issue, when something goes wrong, we immediately relay the results back to ourselves; we take everything personally. The project fell through because I double-checked it and never saw the error. Therefore, the project falling through is now my fault. I did everything I could to uphold the marriage, and I truly gave it my all, but it ended. It must have been my fault. I let my walls down in a relationship and finally let someone in. They chose to leave, while knowing everything about me. I must not have been good enough.

For us believers, life is even more complicated. Have you ever felt like the holy spirit has guided you or opened unreachable doors for you? Have you ever simply *known* that this opportunity was divinely led because you wouldn't have gotten it otherwise? Well, what happens when those doors are shut right in front of you, and your plans come tumbling down? Was God wrong? Was your discernment wrong? There must be something wrong with you, because God can't be wrong. You must have misheard or misinterpreted Him, and now the confidence you have in your discernment is gone. If you can't decide what you want versus what God wants, what a mess that is for a Christian. All of these circumstances, for me, have stemmed from my expectations that if I am closely enough involved in every detail of a situation, when something goes wrong, it must be my fault.

As a human anyways, we aren't able to see the entire story. We see one tree in an entire forest. We see one leaf on that one tree among billions of other leaves that aren't visible to us. I've decided to stop being such a micromanager in my own life because:

1. The closer I get doesn't guarantee that I'll be able to prevent all failures that come my way.
2. I can already only see a tree among the forest. Only God can see it all. Moving in closer isn't going to show me anything more. If anything, it's going to do the opposite.
3. Life is too short to be playing defense constantly.
4. I am more confident when I give "chance" the freedom to be an option.

Let me explain these deeper.

1. The closer I get doesn't guarantee that I'll be able to prevent all failures that come my way.

Whether we like it or not, the formula for this life isn't always as simple as 2+2=4. We can have all the correct variables strewn out in the perfect equation and still not receive the answer we thought we should receive. I think up until I graduated from college, I had the opposite mindset. If I had performed poorly on an exam, it was because I didn't study enough. If a friendship was slipping away, it was because I wasn't investing enough time and effort into it. If I didn't get the job or the internship, it was because I wasn't qualified enough or didn't have enough experience. It was all about working harder, doing more, and being strict with myself. If not, I simply believed that it was all my fault or maybe the fault of the other person involved, but definitely not because of chance.

Post-graduation, my life went through total upheaval, and the things I had poured my heart into didn't end up reaping the results I thought they would. I was in utter disbelief and constantly rationalized everything that was happening by making it all my fault. Granted, I am not perfect, and throughout that process I learned plenty of things that I could have done better; however, overall, if anyone had looked at my playbook they would have sworn I should have won the game.

It was like Kentucky playing Duke in a basketball game, and we (Kentucky) were ahead the entire game. At some parts of the game we even had a comfortable lead. Then we get to the last quarter, and they start catching up without us really noticing. It's a missed three from us and a hit two-pointer for them. Slowly without us realizing, the comfortable lead is now down to two points. There are twelve seconds left, and Duke has the ball. They come down the court and throw up a buzzer-beater, and it goes in. We lose by one point to one of our biggest rivals.

That's exactly how I felt.

Maybe there were some things the team and I could have improved on, but we should have won the game. The odds were in our favor, the talent, the agility, the stamina. We were the better team, but we lost. Maybe that analogy is a stretch, but for me, it's the only way I have been able to understand that sometimes in life, you can be the perfect player, have the better team, and still lose. Life is full of unseen battles, conversations, choices, and even a little bit of luck that decides where our next journey will take us. Stressing, carrying the weight solely on your back, and being overly involved doesn't do anything but crush our confidence when things fall apart and leave us disappointed when the results we thought we deserved don't come to fruition.

2. I can already only see a tree among the forest, while only God can see it all. Moving in closer isn't going to show me anything more; if anything, it's going to do the opposite.

Oftentimes I catch myself only seeing life through the tiny bubble that I am immersed in. Over and over, God has had to remind me that I cannot see the entire picture independently. As I mentioned earlier, I run to the mountains, full speed ahead, hoping that I will finally find the answer I have been looking for by breaking down each and every part of a situation. I go over scenarios in my head, I ask a million questions, I run and run, but the closer I get to analyzing the leaves on a single tree, the less I can see the beauty of the entire mountain range.

There are some instances when we have to stop meddling in God's business and let Him, free will, and—if you believe in it—a little bit of chance, run its course. Up close, the Tetons look like nothing more than boulders of rock, but from far off, they are the most beautiful, unique mountains most have ever laid eyes on.

3. Life is too short to be playing defense constantly.

I must be really missing sports, because I keep coming back to sports references. But in all seriousness, micromanaging your life leads to complete exhaustion. I am continually trying to chase my tail by working for answers that I might not ever receive, preparing myself for excuses for why things didn't work out, and trying to be a total expert on everything I'm involved in so that I will have no reason for failure or room for ignorance.

Doesn't all of that just sound exhausting?

Just as everyone who plays sports knows, defense is critical, but it's also fun to sometimes play a little offense. It's exhilarating to score for your team, to score for yourself if you're playing a one-person sport. It's self-esteem boosting to leave the details behind for a moment and focus on the big picture—to see how far you've come and to trust that the big picture is so much greater than the tiny details.

I don't know if anyone has told you, but you don't have to be an expert on everything. You don't have to be the very best at everything you do. You don't have to give your entire life to one particular thing just to be sure that one thing goes according to plan. You can be multi-passionate. You can make mistakes and be okay. You can totally fail at something and be okay. This life isn't all about how much you can accomplish in the years you have here. And it's also not all about how many people you can make proud of you.

If we are always playing defense, we will never find the courage to try something new and shoot our shot at a different goal. Live a little. Give yourself some grace. Falling down isn't the end of the world as long as you're confident enough to stand back up.

4. I am more confident when I give "chance" the freedom to be an option.
This one is intimidating for even me to admit. I hate chance. I hate knowing that something could go totally wrong and be completely out of my control. I hate knowing that I can't fix everything. But I know that when I have given "chance" a foot in the race, I have felt a weight lifted off me. My expectations go from "If this doesn't work out, it's my fault" to "Because of chance, fate, whatever you want to call it, if this doesn't work out, I don't have to hold total responsibility for it. It's not entirely my fault."

Now, this isn't an excuse to not own up for our losses and shortcomings, but it's a way to show ourselves some grace by understanding that life is made up of more than simply my choices and abilities. By allowing that thought to have a space to live in my mind, I am then confident enough to pursue the task in front of me without carrying the burden of the potential failure before it even happens. Why not give it my all? What do I have to lose? There's a chance that I could fall flat on my face, or there's a chance I could ace this thing, and it still not work out in my favor. That's just a part of life and what makes it exciting. I can choose for "chance" to be my enemy, or I can choose for it to be my friend. Without always blaming myself, I can choose to allow "chance" to take the blame sometimes too, and that's okay.

I always title my chapters "Untitled _" during the process of writing them if I haven't already thought of a title prior. Of course, after I finish, I almost know immediately what to name it and change the name in my outline. For this chapter, I decided to leave it.

Untitled 1.

Throughout our lives, we frequently think we know where we are going, what we are doing, and where we stand regarding who we are. Then, either God, chance, free will, or something else comes in and shows us that we didn't actually know what we thought we did. We were once again staring at the tree, admiring the details, and avoiding everything around us that made up the big picture. We then sponge off the title we thought we had written out for our lives and begin to try again. We take some steps back, admire the new view for what it really is, and keep walking. Sooner or later, we find ourselves once again back in the weeds of life, confused, hurt, and hopeless because we had thought again that we knew.

I think I've decided now to leave my life with the title "Untitled 1."

Until I can become more disciplined at allowing God to be the only one to see my entire life's journey for what it is. He is the only One who can tell my story with the validity and credibility it deserves. Without the Tetons in full view, my description wouldn't be nearly as beautiful. This holds true for my life in God's view as well. The titles I keep guessing at just aren't nearly as good.

TOO OFTEN WE ARE TOLD TO

JUST "LET THE SEASON PASS"

INSTEAD OF BEING TAUGHT HOW

TO BE PRUNED WITHIN THAT

SEASON SO THAT WE WILL BE

BETTER EQUIPPED FOR THE

NEXT WINTER.

ALONE BUT FAR FROM LONELY

To finish up the last half of this book, I took a trip out west to Jackson, Wyoming. I wouldn't say I had "writer's block" at the time. I simply wanted to go on a trip alone for a few reasons, one of them being to get more inspired for this book. I also wanted to clear my head and gather my thoughts without having the distractions I would have at home. I am still processing everything that happened on this trip because going somewhere new for an extended amount of time, alone, will really bring out the subconscious in a person and make those things visible—maybe for the first time in some regard.

As I continue onward with this book, I know I will have revelations stemmed from this trip's memories. If you don't get anything else from this book, I hope you at least develop a yearning for travel and self-discovery—true self-discovery.

I hinted in a previous chapter that doing things alone is one of the few ways to bolden your confidence and to learn about yourself. In this chapter, I want to solidify that thought and give some other practical ways to not only be confident in the person you are but to trust yourself enough to make decisions that will further develop you into the person you want to become.

A couple of days ago I drove into Yellowstone National Park, and although it's only the first few days of October, fall is in full swing there. The evergreens still gleam bright green, but the rest of the landscape is overtaken by hues of orange, brown, yellow, and red. As I drove up the mountain throughout the south entrance, I couldn't help but think how synonymous these trees are to our lives. How we too go through season upon season, and without choice are made to change and morph to fit the mold of that climate.

I'm sure if you look up songs with the title "Seasons," you'll find countless (I can think of two off the top of my head alone). Christians throw around the phrase "it's just a season" every time someone struggles with a circumstance. And even though that may be true, no one ever talks about the changing we do throughout those seasons and how if we want to keep producing good fruit, we have to be willing to adapt.

Too often we are told to just "let the season pass" instead of being taught how to be pruned within that season so that we will be better equipped for the next winter. I continued my drive and saw some trees still with their green leaves, some that were fully yellow, and some that were totally barren. My first thought when I saw the last trees was, "How exposed and vulnerable do they have to feel? A tree without its leaves, being so entirely stripped down of the beauty that we marvel over, how tragic is that?" And then I caught myself and realized, "But *that* is their purpose!"

A tree's purpose isn't to satisfy me with its colorful and vibrant leaves; a tree's purpose is to change and grow and adapt in all circumstances to keep the ecosystem afloat. Its purpose is to produce oxygen for us to breathe, to scatter and multiply, and to do those things it has to do to totally transform each new season. The trees don't care what I think about them; they simply do what they were created to do. I laughed and immediately thought back to the chapter I wrote on learning to love yourself even when the person or people you value the most don't reciprocate that love back to you.

Our job isn't to fit the mold that others have placed on us. I think about my career and how my art minor and dream to be a sculptor don't fit the mold of a corporate employee, but I can do both because I wasn't created to fit the mold of either career entirely. I'm too analytical to be an artist, and I'm too creative to be an analyst—and yet I want to do both. And if we aren't careful, we will slowly get shoved and pushed into a box that we weren't created for. If we don't keep our dreams, passions, and desires in check and at the forefront of our minds, we will begin to start changing to fit into the circumstances right in front of us, whether we truly want that or not.

Many people I know didn't plan on doing the same job they started twenty years ago for the rest of their lives, but they did.

1. Because it became easy.
2. Because they didn't keep their dreams ahead of them.

They left their dreams behind and never decided to pick them back up or change courses and find a new one.

Or maybe it's option 3. Because they thought it was "too late" to start over. The security of where they were outweighed the risk of trying something new—even if that something new could have been what they were created to do.

I am so blessed to have the parents I do, because one of the most important things they have taught me and have lived out fully is that it's never too late to start over. My parents are in their forties (young, I know) and both just graduated with a bachelor's degree. My mom just started a new career last year. My dad is applying for new jobs all around the country, willing to go wherever the wind takes them. At twenty-three, I have no idea where I will be in one year, much less five; I lost the "five-year plan" a month after I graduated from college. However, I am keeping my dreams ahead of me, and I'm taking steps to get to them. And one of those steps is keeping my confidence and trust in myself high. You've heard it before, "If I don't believe in myself, who will?"

If I am always waiting on the season to pass instead of pulling up shortcomings by the root when I'm in a tough season, how will I ever walk through the summer seasons in confidence? If I never strip down the hard stuff, let all the leaves fall off, challenge how gracefully I walk through long periods of suffering, how will I ever truly know the value of a beautiful and fruitful spring? We have to stop being so insecure when it comes to being totally barren in the dark seasons. The most heroic and successful people in history have gone through the darkest seasons of life, but they weren't the ones to simply "let it pass." They made art in the hurt, wrote songs in the pain, received life-changing counseling in the broken, or completely started over by digging up the ghosts that have haunted them for years and made something new with the dust they had left.

Transformation happens when we take the hard, and what could have been defeated in us, and we change our mindset, change our perspective, and transform to better suit our current environment. We study, and we ask God what we need to learn from this, and we come out fighting instead of sitting in the corner waiting for it to pass. Sometimes starting over looks like taking steps backward when truly it's the only way to move forward. If we are doing something wrong, we have to undo/unlearn the wrongness before we can learn to do it right.

Speaking of starting over, another thing I realized as I was driving through Yellowstone, thinking about the trees, is that they change without reluctance.

I think back on just this past year and how many times I realized something needed to change within me or around me, and I dug my heels in and hoped that the feeling would pass. The hard part about introspection is that once you learn the dark and dirty about yourself, you are then responsible for changing it. From the little things you don't like to the big things that you know will change your life in a remarkable way. You can choose to "let awareness be enough" because "that's just the way you are," or you can start the change now.

I mean, for starters, why is it that people get road rage so badly? Maybe the person driving slow has a disability, and they always drive slower just to play it safe? Or maybe on a back road, they just want to enjoy the view? Or in the case of the person speeding at ninety miles per hour, maybe there is an emergency. Or maybe people just suck at driving. I think most of us have been both people in plenty of situations – the turtle and the speed-racer. And in either situation, neither person is in the right or wrong, so why don't we show some grace? Or what about that time you accidentally pulled out in front of someone? You can ask my friends; I rarely ever get road rage these days because I've realized what a waste of energy it is.

Ever since I realized how much I hate getting so worked up over people that have easily been me in a different situation, I decided to just give them all some grace. Maybe they've had a bad day, maybe they're dealing with something urgent, or maybe they just truly suck at driving. Nonetheless, it doesn't matter. And something so small that I have changed my mindset around has had such a positive impact on my days. By not giving other people's driving tendencies the power to change my emotions from good to bad, I have gained a lot more happy moments, enough to add up to full days.

I'm not going to dig into the deeper aspects, but you know what those things are. If you've taken time to challenge yourself, you'll know if you struggle with pride, jealousy, envy, greed, and so on. By this far into the book, you'll know that we all have deeply rooted characteristics that can stem from our childhood that affect how we treat people, how we treat ourselves, and how we live out our day-to-day lives. But the key to correcting all of these things is we have to start permitting ourselves to get it wrong. And ironically, confidence is the key to this. When you are confident in yourself, you know that getting something wrong isn't something that is going to derail you.

There's a difference between being confident in your abilities and being confident in who you are as a person, and one is of astronomical more importance. If you are confident in solely your knowledge of a subject or your ability to do something, learning that you are wrong could be humiliating. Having confidence that stems from your soul, from who you are within? No incorrect behavior or thought process could ever derail that. When a person is confident because they know they were created for a purpose, every incorrect thought or correction they receive from someone is simply leading them closer to the truth, closer to their ideal self, and closer to that purpose.

We have to start giving ourselves permission to change our minds when we are presented with new information. When we are freed from that sickening feeling in our stomach when we find out we were wrong, when we start saying thank you for help and correction, when we start challenging our own ideologies and beliefs, we will exponentially gain confidence. Nothing wipes away insecurity like a person who isn't afraid to be wrong and change course.

The trees know their purpose would not be achieved without change. Once again, the potential you have for growth is dependent on the amount of humility you allow yourself to feel. The Redwood trees in California aren't there today because they refused to change. They are hundreds of years old and the size of cars because they continuously adapted and grew into who they were created to be. Too many of us stop short and never see what we were capable of in this life. As Wayne Dyer once said, "Don't die with the music still left inside of you."

The last thing I want to share is another glimpse through my social media lens. I wrote this post as soon as I got back from Wyoming, and I meant every word. I hope that if I've convinced you enough to take steps into realizing your worth and confidence, you'll read this post and maybe even start planning your own solo trip somewhere, whether it be for just a weekend or even a couple of weeks.

"What progress, you ask, have I made? I have begun to be a friend to myself." - Seneca

Traveling alone has shown me so many things about myself. All the time to think. All the time to ask questions. All the time to see where my wandering mind chooses to go.

As I was driving through the Tetons a few days ago, I looked in the rearview mirror at myself and laughed at how crazy I am sometimes. All the way out here, no cell phone service, basically camping every day, & all by myself. What was I thinking??

I laughed & drove on & as time went, I noticed myself dreaming bigger dreams, thinking about books I wanted to read, places I wanted to visit, new things I wanted to try. I was taking notes constantly on new sculptures I wanted to make when I got back, how I wanted to finish my book, & tiny epiphanies that finally made certain things make sense.

Where had all of this been before??

It's amazing what our minds are capable of coming up with when we give them a break from trying to entertain other people.

I drove on & was more excited than ever to chase these big dreams I have. Grad school. My book. An artist. An amateur archer. A better friend. A good mother one day. A wife that challenges him big but encourages him even bigger. A world traveler. An animal whisperer. A winery owner. A brand creator. A God-fearing woman who shakes the feet of those who don't know His name.

I started making plans & deciding my next steps. It was like I was helping a friend find the fire within her again. Instead of scrutinizing myself for the wrong turns and the failed attempts, I was finally treating myself like a best friend. Giving grace & encouragement & inspiration every step of the way.

Travel alone sometimes, you guys. Your soul is waiting for you to do it."

I'VE LEARNED THAT OUR TRUE SELVES COME NOT IN THE BATTLE THEMSELVES, BUT IN THE WAITING, IN THE PREPARATION, AND IN THE SOUL-SEARCHING IN-BETWEENS WHERE WE FEEL LIKE WE HAVE BEEN FORGOTTEN.

FIERCE

I hope by the time you've made it to the end of this book, you've realized that reaching your potential by pursuing self-awareness, growth, intentionality, and confidence isn't something that is freely given or stumbled upon; these things take work.

Serious work.

It takes obedience, perseverance, and maybe even a little bit of long-suffering. It takes apologizing, maybe to others, and likely to yourself. It takes the willingness to be knocked down while choosing to get up again, stronger and more resolute than ever before. It takes humility, lots of humility. It takes willingness to be wrong, willingness to change, and willingness to learn from every person smarter and farther along in their journey than you. It takes getting out of your comfort zone, doing things you don't desire doing, and sacrificing your well-being for others.

In the end, it simply takes work.

I can't speak for every generation, but I know my generation is great at taking instead of giving, cowering down when we should be standing up, taking time off when we should be putting in work, and expecting everyone else to take on our responsibilities for us. We let others research for us, we let the media tell us what to believe, we let others work so that we can receive the benefits, and somehow we still believe that we deserve every good thing this world has to offer.

Purpose is one of the few things that can't be paid for, for you; you have to buy it yourself. It's time that we all stand up and choose to take responsibility not for what everyone else is doing but for what *we* are doing. It's time that we do some intense introspection, ask what we can do to help, and get back to work so that we can begin to add value to our lives as well as the lives of those around us. When we are all doing our part to improve ourselves, chase the truth, and make selfless decisions, we all win. Every single one of us, by sacrificially giving our best selves to those around us, we all end up winning. By taking the time to learn our purpose, learn our passions, learn our flaws, learn our strengths, we will not only become more satisfied and joy-filled humans, but we will also be giving our best self to society. We will all be putting our absolute best foot forward for those around us.

One of the greatest books that I have ever read is *Man's Search for Meaning* by the Holocaust survivor Viktor Frankl. A man who had every right to feel like he deserved the world after what he had been through, he nevertheless had nothing to ask for but everything to give back. Throughout this book, Frankl discusses how when everything is stripped from a person, you have the choice to see life as meaningless or still meaningful. Day in and day out, he spent years starving to death in a concentration camp where he witnessed thousands of people die at the hands of the Nazi regime. In one part of the book, he discusses how he could look at a man and know if he was soon going to die. In the camps, the prisoners were occasionally given cigarettes, and Frankl explained that the norm was to save your cigarettes for a bad day. Every day was bad, but cigarettes were typically saved for the worst and most gruesome of days. He then goes on to say that if he saw a man smoke his last cigarette, he knew that within two days the man would be gone; he had lost all will to live. As a psychiatrist in his former life, Frankl watched the behavior of his fellow prisoners and observed their mental and emotional states throughout his time in the camps. Spoiler alert: after Frankl gets out of the camps and is set free, he has many other emotional experiences that he has to overcome.

He says, "A man who for years had thought he had reached the absolute limit of all possible suffering now found that suffering has no limits, and that he could suffer still more, and still more intensely."

Viktor Frankl, throughout his unimaginable suffering, as well as my own life experiences, taught me that in this life we get a choice. No matter if our lives take us on beautiful, scenic routes or through the gas chambers of Auschwitz, in both scenarios we are given a choice to see life as purposeful and worthy of being lived, or not. The will to live isn't based on our circumstances but on our willingness to give this life a piece of us we believe it deserves.

Frankl puts it best: "We had to learn ourselves and, furthermore, we had to teach the despairing men, that it did not really matter what we expected from life, but rather what life expected from us."

Yesterday morning, my grandfather passed away. And although "the purpose of our lives" has been a cloud over my head throughout the entire process of writing this book, I feel the weight of it heavier today than any other day yet. My grandfather was diagnosed with cancer nine days ago, and yesterday, he passed. As quickly as he had gotten a cough, his spirit was lifted from his body and flown to an afterlife, I believe, to be much better than the one we have here. In the blink of an eye we are nothing more than either a legacy to those who knew us or another unfinished project that was left behind many years ago or maybe never even started.

We cannot simply dumb down our life's purpose based on the veering roads we chose to take or the doors that were presented to us to walk through. There isn't one specific purpose for all of us. We aren't all dealt the same cards, nor are we all expected to endure the same level of suffering. Our attitudes toward what we owe to life must be a yearning we never lose while we are here. I found this excerpt to be one of the most meaningful in the book:

> Life ultimately means taking the responsibility to find the right answer to its problems and to fulfill the tasks which it constantly sets for each individual. These tasks, and therefore the meaning of life, differ from man to man, and from moment to moment. Thus it is impossible to define the meaning of life in a general way. Questions about the meaning of life can never be answered by sweeping statements. "Life" does not mean something vague, but something very real and concrete. They form man's destiny, which is different and unique for each individual. No man and no

destiny can be compared with any other man or any other destiny. No situation repeats itself, and each situation calls for a different response. Sometimes the situation in which a man finds himself may require him to shape his own fate by action. At other times, it is more advantageous for him to make use of an opportunity for contemplation and to realize assets in this way. Sometimes man may be required simply to accept fate, to bear his cross. Every situation is distinguished by its uniqueness, and there is always only one right answer to the problem imposed by the situation at hand. When a man finds that his destiny is to suffer, he will have to accept his suffering as his task; his single and unique task. He will have to acknowledge the fact that even in suffering he is unique and alone in the universe. No one can relieve him of his suffering or suffer in his place. His unique opportunity lies in the way in which he bears his burden.

Although you may have picked up this book as an intentional action to better improve yourself, encourage yourself, or do something else for yourself, reaching your highest level of understanding, seeing the true rawness of who you are, and developing your inner consciousness through the four pillars laid out in this book aren't simply means to give you a greater satisfaction with yourself.

We *owe* our best selves to this life.

We owe life the journey of pursued purpose, pursued passion, and a relentless determination to never give up on it. We owe life the most chiseled and molded, varnished and polished version of ourselves. We have purpose whether we choose to see it or not. We have passions, abilities, goals, and dreams set inside of us whether we choose to discover them or not. We have moments of suffering, brokenness, disappointments beyond what we think we can bear, whether we chose to walk through those moments with our heads held high or not. We don't stumble upon dreams. We don't accidentally find meaning for this life. We are warriors who have the choice to equip ourselves for battle in this life or let our guard down so that the enemy can come in at any point and overcome us. As the dialogue between Watson and Holmes goes:

Dr. Watson: "How did you see that?"
Sherlock Holmes: "Because I was looking for it."

The challenges of life are going to come, whether we are prepared for them or not. Opportunities are also going to come, whether we are prepared for them or not. So we must be looking in anticipation, waiting for our time to pay our debts to this life and simultaneously feel our purpose and gratification for living rise within us.

I've learned that our true selves come not in the battle themselves, but in the waiting, in the preparation, and in the soul-searching in-betweens where we feel like we have been forgotten. When we are being pushed, challenged, sought after, entrusted, and given a task set before us, we finally feel valued again. And in those moments before and after the highs and lows of life, we need to be sharpening our knives, loading our guns, and training for a better comeback the next go around. We have to dig into self-awareness, fight for growth, uncomfortably become more intentional, and choose to invest in our confidence. The battleground isn't always where you are, and it isn't far off in the distance of where you want to be. The battleground is in the in-between. The transformation happens in the in-between.

A lion isn't taught how to be fierce. It learns on its own because it knows what it was destined to become—and in its world, you either become who you were destined to be, or you die trying.

"HE ISN'T SAFE. BUT
HE'S GOOD. HE'S THE
KING, I TELL YOU."

- C.S. LEWIS

FINAL PIECE OF THE PUZZLE

It was the beginning of December and I had just clicked "submit" and closed my laptop. My very first manuscript was now in the hands of someone else, my editor, and I was to simply sit and wait patiently to hear back on the changes she thought should be made.

My stomach was in knots and I couldn't decide if I was holding back tears due to excitement or nervousness or both. "This is actually happening," I thought to myself.

Eighteen months.

Eighteen long months of keeping these pages a private part of my life. Eighteen months of wrestling with not being good enough to be an author, not having the right words, not being able to articulate my thoughts accurately, and not knowing if I should publish this at all or just keep it to myself.

If I'm being honest, this book gave me purpose in one of the most painful seasons of my life. It was a vice, a friend, and a way to show life that I wasn't finished with it just yet, a way to show God I wasn't finished with Him just yet, and a way for God to show ME that He wasn't finished with me just yet. So why wouldn't I selfishly keep it for only myself? I had gotten what I needed out of it and if I kept it tucked away safely, no more of me would be exposed to the world. I wouldn't have to worry about negative reviews or DNFs (people implying the book was not intriguing enough so they "Did Not Finish" it). Most importantly, these vulnerable moments I mention in the book, those wouldn't have to be put on display for everyone to see. My emotions could reside safely within me and within the pages of this un-published manuscript. *Safely*.

That's the word that changed everything. Because I'm not a "safe" person. I don't play life *safe*. I don't love safe. I don't stay home where I'm safe. I don't have safe conversations. My career moves haven't been safe. Even the crazy things I order off the menu at restaurants aren't safe (I'm not a chicken tenders and fries kind of girl. I'll take the most interesting sounding item on the menu and hope I like it). My life is defined by risk. Time and time again I take risks. I take risks on love. I take risks when I'm traveling to places most people wouldn't dare to go. I take risks in my conversations with people. I take risks in studying my opposing views, challenging them to change my mind on politics, religion, music taste, and anything else I've done my research on or have an opinion on.

It's true that maybe the times I have been the most hurt, the most knocked off my feet and devastated, are due to risks that could have been avoided. Like that time a friend and I were trespassing in an abandoned art building, scaled onto the roof, and then had to climb down a twenty-foot tree to flee from the cops on foot. We had poison ivy all over our bodies for weeks and I swear we ran three miles that night to get away (it was so epic). He and I probably should've never been there in the first place, but, off the record, I still don't regret it. The deeper risks that have caused emotional, spiritual, or mental hurt are the ones I'm referring to more. But even with those, it's also true that my most meaningful memories, my most impactful conversations, my most cherished travel adventures, and my most pivotal, life-changing moments have also been due to the risks that I'm so thankful I took a chance on. How could I miss this opportunity to share something that just might incline other people to live their lives the same way? We aren't called to be safe. We're called to be fierce.

C.S. Lewis writes in *The Lion, The Witch, and the Wardrobe*:

"Aslan is a lion—the Lion, the great Lion."

"Ooh," said Susan. "I'd thought he was a man. Is he quite safe? I shall feel rather nervous about meeting a lion"

"Safe?" said Mr. Beaver. "Who said anything about safe? 'Course he isn't safe. But He's good. He's the King, I tell you."

Fast forward a few weeks after I submitted my manuscript, and some of my closest friends and I are in Hawaii. The entire first week I couldn't stop thinking about how incredible it would be to have the cover of my book shot here in Hawaii. The mountains scream risk, challenge, triumph, and strength. The continuous fog hovering over them tells a story of mystery and potential danger. The sun shines redemption, glory, and joy onto anyone willing to step outside. The ocean beckons you in with its beauty and grace but tells you it's also not safe.

This is the place. This is where it all comes together. This is the final piece of the puzzle.

Luckily, a friend of mine on the trip has his own photography and videography business. When I shared with him that I wanted him to try and get the shot for my book, we were both giddy with excitement. I told him that I was just trusting that it would happen on its own without being forced. I had no idea if I wanted to be on the cover or if it just be a beautiful scene from Hawaii. I had no other ideas about what the cover should look like, but I was trusting that an opportunity would present itself and I would just know when we had the shot. I had a good feeling and continued praying that God would help this whole thing come together.

Days pass and it's our last full day in Hawaii. Determined to get the photo we wanted, Alex (the photographer friend) and I decided to drive around the island that day and see what we could find. I promise you, we looked up three scenic locations and every single one we went to had huge gates closing off the entrance. I started to lose hope, but once again, it was time to take a risk. No more playing it safe. (By the way, I don't condone trespassing. I am simply telling my story and risk seems to be a recurring theme here.)

The last park we went to had gates at the front, so we parked the car and walked over. You could see past the fence, and there were a couple of people walking their dogs and riding bikes, also ignoring the closed gate. Alex looks at me and says, "Let's try it. We walk as far along this road as we can and see if we can get the shot." So we did. He let me look over them quickly on his camera and I loved them! I was so excited. The look on my face screamed *fierce* and in that moment, I was so proud to have been entrusted to be the author of this book. We got back in our car and began driving to pick up our friends from the beach. Along the way I received an Instagram message from someone I had never met and only spoken to a couple of times, but who had become a social media friend due to our shared passion for travel. The message said this: "Crouching Lion is a local hike [on Oahu]. There's no real route without a local so befriend someone who's done it. Top notch views of the bay and side of the island."

I read the text out loud to Alex and we agreed to try and convince our friends to find a way to do this hike with us. It took some convincing, but we found a couple of blogs online that outlined the hike and were on our way. I looked it up and found this article by Thomas Burton. I didn't share this with the group at the time, and you'll understand why.

> "This trail is not for the faint of heart or those easily scared of heights. The crouching lion trail is a 4 mile loop with an elevation gain of 2,000 feet. The elevation gains and losses are near the beginning and the end of the trail. The middle of the trail is where the dangerous knife-like ridges are."

"Crouching Lion," I thought. "How weird that the last line of my book refers to the fierceness of a lion and now we are on our way to do this 'highly dangerous,' off-the-grid hike with that name."

I knew then that God was up to something; Aslan was on the move.

We hiked, we climbed, and we repelled up the mountain with ropes. We slipped, we crawled, and we walked alongside the ridgeline of the mountain, finally coming to the top. The blogs I found online about "Crouching Lion" say that there is a rock near the top that looks like a lion crouching, about to pounce on its prey.

Sure enough, we looked across the mountain and you could see a lion-looking figure lying on the very tip of a steep edged rock. "That's it!" I said. To the others it sounded like I was talking about the lion, and in a way, I was. But I meant Aslan, not this lion. Tears began to puddle in my eyes, but the wind ferociously wiped them away with each one that fell. It was so loud from the wind, you could barely hear the person next to you. Every video I have from that hike has useless audio once we got to the top. It was as if you could hear the call of danger.

One wrong step, and you were gone. But one right step and you were overlooking, arguably, one of the most beautiful sights in the world.

I looked up, with a heart full of humility and reverence, and whispered, "Thank you." I knew then that everything would work out. It always works out.

It wasn't a coincidence I received the Instagram message that day from a stranger. It wasn't a coincidence that my amazingly talented friend Alex was on this trip with me. It wasn't a coincidence that the name of this hike was "Crouching Lion." It wasn't a coincidence that all the other scenic locations were closed. It wasn't a coincidence that God waited until the very last minute to show Himself. It wasn't a coincidence that three of my very best friends were with me to share that special moment, the moment I knew I found the missing piece of the puzzle. The moment where my purpose for writing this book came together. The moment when I realized how important risk is. How important trust is. How important faith is. How important patience is. How important the battleground is. And how important it is for us to get back up and climb the dangerous, treacherous mountain with your friends alongside you, in order to finally see the beauty of life again. Your heart is racing, the air you're breathing feels like the freshest air in the world. Your blood is pumping, and your heart is beating fast. Your eyes are wide open not wanting to miss a thing. Your legs are shaking but they're just as eager to see what's next, so they keep stepping for you.

Reaching the top of the mountain that day was like going home. I had never been there, but it was as if God met me there, as if Aslan was waiting for me at the top of Crouching Lion, just so that He could throw off every insecurity, every last bit of pain and hurt I was still healing from and say, "Well done." The joy was overwhelming. The weight of His glory was too heavy, I could only hold it for a moment. But what an honor to worship a God who shows up in the most treacherous and dangerous conditions to tell us that we are safe with Him.

We aren't called to be safe, but the irony is that, in the hands of the most untamed, unsafe lion, we are more secure and safe than anywhere else.

"He isn't safe. But He's good. He's the King, I tell you."
— C.S. Lewis

If you're looking for the photo, turn your book over to the back cover. You'll find it there. It was a moment too precious to be printed on the front. A moment I will cherish forever, but one I want to keep hidden a little while longer.

AFTERWORD

I truly don't know where to begin other than by simply saying thank you.

Thank you for taking the time to read my words, hear my thoughts, and gain insight into my vulnerable moments that I never thought would be put on paper.

This book was written during some of my darkest days but was also the conduit that led me into some of my brightest ones.

If I could go back in time I would eagerly shake the hands of C.S. Lewis, Viktor Frankl, J.R.R. Tolkien, Maurice Nicoll, Vincent Van Gogh, Corrie Ten Boom, and many others who have inspired me and given me the tools to live an extraordinary life, search for truth, and chase my passions without looking back.

Thank you to my parents and dear friends who have never stopped believing in me and who cheer me on with every next crazy idea or adventure.

Lastly, thank you to younger Katlyn. For enduring what she did, figuring out who she was, and giving life a chance again. She came back more resilient and fierce than ever before.

This book is for her.

ACKNOWLEDGEMENTS

Thank you to the Great Lion himself for instilling this dream in me almost 2 years ago now and for showing me that pain may just be the primary fuel you need to find your purpose. Our relationship hasn't always been easy, but it's real and it's good. You're all I truly need. Ephesians 3:20.

Thank you, once again, to my parents. They have sacrificed so much for me, more than I could ever repay them for. They inspire me and show me that it's never too late to start over or to try something new.

Thank you to my great-grandparents who are no longer earth-side but are now walking the streets of heaven. My entire life you both chose me time and time again. You made me feel as if I could take on the world, head-first, and with fire in my eyes. I love you and miss you more than you know.

My Nana. A woman of God who found her passion, pursued it fiercely, and works harder than anyone I know. You taught me that nothing good ever comes easy.

Everyone else in my family who had little but gave much. I didn't realize it as a child, but I promise I do now. Thank you.

My best friends. You know who you are. You've shown up

for me in my darkest of days while gently and patiently walking through the storm with me – out of the shadows and into the light. It's been so long. I've changed more than I ever thought possible. & somehow you all still love me the same, if not more, than you did before. I wouldn't be here without you and I mean that.

Wes & Nina Mullins. God knew what He was doing when He led me to you. You both have impacted my life in ways I get too emotional to put onto paper. Thank you for believing in me. Thank you for being my friends, my mentors, and my second family all in one.

My Cambodian Family. I flew to Cambodia and from the first day I met you in your village, Vuthy, Connie, and Malachi, you treated me like I was family – like I had been family since birth. You showed me what true sacrifice, true servanthood, and true selfless love looks like. I will never forget that, and I promise I will see you soon.

Dave Osborne. From calling you professor to career mentor to now friend, I have so much to thank you for. You saw potential in me years ago and never let me give up or think less of myself. You have been in my corner since the beginning.

My friend, Alex Thompson (Thompson Audio/Visions), who photographed the cover photo while we were in Hawaii. The cover is all the more special because of where we were and who we were with. I can't say thank you enough.

Brooks, my editor, Vanessa, my cover designer and typesetter, and Jeff, my proofreader. Thank you all for every minute you spent working to make this vision of mine come to life.

Last but not least, my Roman Beau. You have turned my crying into laughing more times than I can count. You were by my side every step of the way with this book. All the late nights writing and editing, you were always there by my feet. My life is so much sweeter because I have you, and the best part of my day is coming home to your fluffy tail wagging, greeting me at the door.